STOLEN YEARS

By the same author:

CARETAKERS, *the Forgotten People*
PLATITUDES, *You are not me!*
DON'T SHOOT! *My life is valuable*

Book covers are reproductions of
the author's oil paintings

STOLEN YEARS

In my little corner of the world

Maita Floyd

Manufactured in the United States of America. Published by Eskualdun Publishers, P.O. Box 50266, Phoenix, AZ 85076. Phone: (602) 893-2394, (800) 848-1192, Fax: (602) 893-9225.

Publisher's Cataloging in Publication
(prepared by Quality Books Inc.)
Floyd, Maita, 1924-
Stolen Years : in my little corner of the world / Maita Floyd.

p. cm.
Preassigned LCCN: 95-60583
ISBN: 0-9620599-4-3

1. Pays Basque (France)—History. 2. World War, 1939-1945—Underground movements—France—Pays Basque. I. Title.

611.B318F56 1995   944.7'90'816
                                     QBI95-20149

Edited by
Gerry Benninger

Book design by
SageBrush Publications
Tempe, Arizona

Cover design by
Carlos Gonzalez
Phoenix, Arizona

To

The American GIs who gave their lives in 1944
to save me from Nazi slavery

and

to the French Basques who died as a consequence of
helping allied pilots, crew members, escaped prisoners,
political escapees and Jews cross the
Pyrénées Mountains to Spain.

ACKNOWLEDGMENTS

Many individuals have contributed in significant ways to this book. Their names have been changed to protect their privacy.

Merci for their recollections to my sisters and beloved tutor/governess *Mademoiselle* Durcudoy whose friendship and support encompassed sixty years. She died before the book was completed. They helped me turn the dusty pages of the past. We sometimes encountered a catalog without definite dates.

Thanks to a very important and special person, my editor, Gerry Benninger, past president and now board member of the Arizona Authors' Association; dear friend Gwen Henson, SageBrush Publications, typesetter and book designer; and Carlos Gonzalez, cover designer. Many thanks to Charles P. Arnot, retired ABC news correspondent who agreed to write *Stolen Years'* preface and to all my reviewers.

Appreciation to the publications for permission to quote: National Geographic Society and Time Inc. In France: Editions Milan, Luz Media and Father Gaztambide pastor of Saint-Jean-de-Luz Catholic Church.

I am grateful for the unending support of my mentor, John McComish, owner of the Little Professor Bookstore in Phoenix, Arizona.

And especially, in my little corner of the world, my friend Bette Derivan who patiently read and reread my manuscript.

In this book, people are as war made them. War is the tale of hate, also of human endurance and survival.

–Maita Floyd

One faces the future with one's past.

–Pearl S. Buck

ABOUT THE AUTHOR

After a thirty-year airline career, Maita Floyd retired in the Ahwatukee area of Phoenix, Arizona. Her writing career began after her husband's death. She devotes much of her time to community service as a Victim/Witness advocate and Hospice volunteer. Maita is a member of the Arizona Governor's Commission on Violence Against Women Task Force.

In 1989, Maita represented Arizona as a Congressional Senior Citizen Intern in Washington, D.C. Since 1990 her name has been listed in Who's Who of American Women and the World.

Maita's many affiliations include the American Legion Auxiliary, Arizona Authors' Association, American Business Women Association and Impact for Enterprising Women.

Maita has been interviewed on numerous television and radio talk shows. She lectures nationwide and in Canada on the topics of her books: caregiving, grief, domestic violence, the long-term aftereffects of victimization and now on her personal experiences as a teenager during the German occupation of France Basque region.

A talented artist, Maita can often be found in front of her easel. She finds time to enjoy her favorite sport of tennis and is active in an entertainers' group.

PREFACE

This fascinating volume rolls back the calendar to World War II and gives a revealing insight into the trials and challenges of one of the least-known minorities—the European Basques.

The wartime chronicle is related by an observant and curious teen-age Basque girl, Maita Branquet, whose parents own and operate an eighty-five room hotel in the quaint summer resort of Saint-Jean-de-Luz, nestled on the Bay of Biscay.

Maita is only fifteen years old when the heavily-armed Germans swarm across her native France and requisition her family's hotel as a rest area for their troops. Maita and her family leave their hotel quarters and move to a villa on a farm not far away.

Then begins a deadly game of cat-and-mouse between the local Basque population and the German invaders. Maita becomes involved with the French Resistance as a messenger on her trusty bicycle.

Reporting from what she calls "my little corner of the world," Maita tells how the cruel Gestapo retaliated after the Allied invasion in Normandy by arresting local underground members and sending them to concentration camps where many died.

At war's end, she observes somewhat bitterly: "My teenage years were now over...stolen...never to be replaced, but not my youth and spirit."

And so, despite parental objection, in November 1946 Maita sailed to the United States, to launch a new life...the only one of seven Branquet children to break with family and Basque tradition.

This is a book that will make you cheer for resistance fighters and weep with Maita over the loss of fellow Basques to Nazi cruelty.

It is a story of tender family remembrances, and equally harsh in recalling the brutal German occupation. Truly an historical gem.

—*Charles P. Arnot, Retired ABC News correspondent,*
Foreign correspondent for 35 years including WWII European
and Pacific theaters, Author of Don't Kill the Messenger

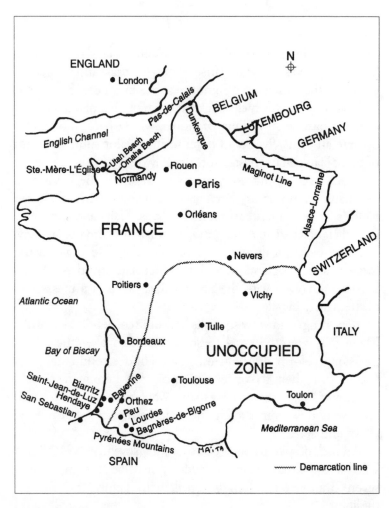

Map of France

Prologue

Sweet is the remembrance of troubles when you are
in safety.

—Euripides

A car door slammed!

"*Jawohl! Herr Oberleutnant.*"

The already detested guttural words were coming from
the sidewalk in front of the hotel. They startled me out of
my reverie. I had been dreaming of the beach, swimming
and the coolness of the sea caressing my suntanned skin.
Instead, I was stuck behind my parents' hotel reception
desk.

Heavy hobnailed footsteps hit the entrance tiles. When
I looked up, an impressively tall German officer with a
determined jaw, and an air of smugness came into my range
of vision. He was wearing an impeccable uniform. He
abruptly stopped in front of the desk and clicked his heels.
His arm extended in the ramrod Nazi salute, symbol of
complete, unconditional obedience to the *Führer*, he
shouted, "*Heil, Hitler!*"

I was shocked! Since the beginning of the occupation four months ago, June 1940, I had not seen a German this close. Without another sound passing his thin lips, he handed me a paper, clicked his heels again, turned around and left. Bewildered, I scanned the official looking document written in French. I could not believe what I read. DISBELIEF! HORROR!

Forgetting my duties, I left the desk unattended looking for my parents, screaming at the top of my lungs, "Papa, Maman."

I found them sitting peacefully in our living quarters. Papa was reading the paper and Maman knitting which she did not do often because she was always busy with the task of running a large hotel. After my dramatic entrance, with a rustle of paper, annoyed Papa looked up.

"*Sacrebleu* (sacred blue)! What is going on? Can't you behave like a young lady? The clients are going to think that we are raising a bunch of unruly children."

Maman, frowning and showing her own disapproval, had dropped her knitting on her lap. After Papa's reprimand she added, "Really, Maita, be reasonable!"

Silently, I handed the document to Papa. As he was reading he turned ashen. Slowly he got up like the weight of the world had just fallen on his shoulders. With a slightly trembling hand, Papa passed the document to Maman who had been looking at him puzzled. She glanced at it, "Oh! *Mon Dieu* (Oh! My God)!" Maman gasped, putting her hand over her mouth. The paper fell to the floor, lying between the three of us like pestilence. It was more than mere German propaganda, it was a requisition order:

"Within twenty-four hours Hôtel de la Poste must be vacated and left in perfect working order, the employees must remain. An officer will come tomorrow morning for final inspection."

It was bad enough that after the shocking defeat of France by the Germans, my hometown, Saint-Jean-de-Luz, was located in the occupied zone. Now, with a piece of paper, we were being thrown out of the hotel; the only home I had ever known. That document meant only one word, *raus* (out), was going to drastically change our lives and rob me of my teenage years.

My world was crumbling!

Who was the cause of it?

Where did it all begin?

In September, 1939, a chain of events began that was going to convulse Europe, throwing it into a most horrible war. Without provocation and to the consternation of Europe, Nazi forces brutally attacked Poland. The *Wehrmacht* (German Army) poured east, deep into the country. Shocks reverberated throughout the world. The invasion of Poland engineered by Hitler's evil mind and madness was the spark of the most vicious of wars yet known, WWII (World War Two).

The 1918 armistice between France and Germany had only lasted a little more than twenty years. During the previous 133 years France and Germany had not been able to live very long at peace with each other. In 1806 Napoléon crushed the Prussians, and in 1870 Napoléon III was defeated by the Prussians. By January, 1871 Paris was under siege, the starving Parisians tragically surrendered. Then

La Grande Guerre (The big war) of 1914-18 was supposed to have ended conflicts between the Germans and the French. All these previous wars had been fought in north-east France at the border between the two countries.

Europe, and later many other world countries, was driven into a horrible world wide, devastating war, sparked by the invasion of Poland. Hitler needed vital space for his country of more than eighty million Germans. His demonic orders were to kill without pity all men, women and children in Poland.

In March 1939 the French and British governments had guaranteed the protection of the Polish Republic. Both countries mobilized after asking Germany to pull its troops out of Poland. From the United States, President Roosevelt pleaded for peace.

Front cover of Hôtel de la Poste promotional booklet.

I had just turned fifteen, until then my life had been peaceful and without material needs. In 1920, my parents, Louis and Félicie Branquet had acquired a hotel and restaurant, Hôtel de la Poste, situated in the lovely, quaint summer resort town of Saint-Jean-de-Luz, strategically located on the main road from Paris to Madrid. Through two decades of hard work they had a thriving hotel business, with a reputation in Western Europe for good food, excellent service, and genteel hospitality.

Oil painting by the author of Saint-Jean-de-Luz with the Pyrénées Mountains in the background.

My hometown, Saint-Jean-de-Luz, is surrounded by breathtaking scenery; mountains, the sea, and a river, *La Nivelle*. The town is nestled on the Atlantic Bay of Biscay on the rugged, southwest Basque coastline, ten miles north of the Spanish border. The natural bay is cool green more than blue due to the seaweed. It was a vacation spot enjoyed mostly by the French during the summers and English during the winters. During the summer months the sandy beach, then as now, was prized by the vacationers who enjoy swimming in the calm bay. The beach was dotted with colorful canvas tents used for changing clothes and by people who wanted to avoid sunburns. On the boardwalk ice cream vendors still attract the young.

Summertime Saint-Jean-de-Luz beach.

Late afternoons, vacationers clogged the narrow streets looking for souvenirs, *Basque bérets* (flat, round wool caps), hand-made *espadrilles* (rope-sole sandals) and other goods in the multitude of souvenir shops. Tea shops selling delicious pastries, macaroons and marzipan did a brisk business.

Early evenings, some vacationers joined the *Luziens* (residents of Saint-Jean-de-Luz) to watch the noisy arrival of the fishing fleet and the unloading of the day's catch: tuna, sardines, eel, squid, flounder and sole. As they left the harbor, they had a choice of regional dishes at excellent restaurants which line the centuries' old streets winding past the church. *Chipirons*, squid cooked in their black ink, is one favorite; another is *Piperade*, omelette with ham, tomatoes, green hot pepper, pimentos, or chicken *à la Basquaise*. *Gâteau Basque* (cake) gave the meals a finishing touch. All of it accompanied by local wine.

Three times a week the local oompah brass band, its members wearing red *bérets*, played in the middle of the Louis XIV town square which is encircled by outdoor cafes. Besides the popular tunes, the band played folkloric Basque dance tunes, the *Arin-Arin* and the *Fandango*. Young men and women wearing Basque espadrilles, arms in the air, danced the intricate rapid steps and spun to their hearts' content. On Sunday nights at eleven, before the traditional confetti battle started, immense bags were purchased by the *Luziens* and vacationers wanting to participate. People sitting at the cafes needed to protect their drinks from being filled with confetti. This mock battle was followed by the grand entrance of the exciting *torro de fuego* (bull of fire). Lights were extinguished in the square, then two men, carrying a wooden bull with fireworks shooting from it, ran through the crowd amidst laughter and squealing. The evening was climaxed by fireworks ending in the display of a crown shooting to the stars. "Oooohs and aaaaahs" came from the mesmerized crowd.

Several excellent golf courses, as well as tennis courts, were at the vacationers' disposal. They also could watch Basque games of *pelota* (ball games) played *esku* (barehanded) or with a *palancha* (short handled, wooden racket) or with a *chistera* (long curved wicker basket solidly attached to the player's hand in a leather glove). The *pilotaris* (players) are dressed in white pants and short-sleeved shirts, their feet in *espadrilles*. Teams were recognized by ribbons of different colors attached to their left shoulders. In the thirties these games were only played in the Basque region. One game, *errebote* (rebot), was played every Sunday behind the Hôtel de la Poste in an open air court called *fronton*. It is an intricate, fast game. When the ball is missed, a referee on the side of the court marks the spot with a branch, at the same time singing the point in Basque. Tourists and local people filled the bleachers, their heads moving in unison to follow the ball which could reach a speed of 150 miles per hour. When the church bells rang the noon hour, the game stopped, everyone stood up, men removed their *bérets*. It was time to pray the Angelus, an old Catholic custom of bowing in prayer at six in the morning, noon and six at night. All Basque towns and villages had their *frontons*, usually near the church.

Game of errebote *played with* chisteras.

The Pyrénées Mountains make a natural border between France and Spain. The lush, dense western Pyrénées,
covered with oak trees, thick green ferns, and thorny furze
turn into rolling hills and lovely valleys before vanishing
abruptly into the storm swept Atlantic Ocean.

Access roads between the two countries can only be
found on either side of the Pyrénées Mountains, one on
the Atlantic in the West, the other on the Mediterranean
in the east. The Western side is the most direct route. Other
accesses are through high mountain passes. Most of them
are arduous and used only by *contrebandiers* (smugglers).
To the Basques, smuggling is no sin, neither is it illegal. It
is said one can't stop them, it's in their blood. Common
belief in France concedes that the best *contrebandiers* are
found in the Basque region on both sides of the Pyrénées.
They know the mountains so well that border customs
agents can seldom catch them. One has to really know the
terrain to find the way through the dense ferns that make
excellent cover.

The Basque region consists of seven provinces that
straddle the Pyrénées Mountains. Three are in France and
four in Spain. The coat of arms reads, *Zazpiak-Bat* (seven
into one). Many French Basques pride themselves on being
Basque first and French second. We are an ancient, most
fascinating race that has been called the *mystery people*. The
origins of the white-skinned Basques have perplexed eth-
nologists and are lost in remote prehistory.

"The most distinctive members of the European branch
of the human tree are the Basques of France and Spain.
They show unusual patterns of several genes, including the
highest rate of the RH-negative blood type. Their language

is of unknown origin and cannot be placed within any standard classification. And the fact that they live in the region adjoining the famous Lascaux and Altamira caves, which contain vivid paintings from Europe's early hunter-gatherers, leads Cavalli-Sforza to tantalizing conclusions:

'The Basques are extremely likely to be the most direct descendants of the Cro-Magnon people, among the first modern humans in Europe.'"[1]

"About 9,000 years ago, soon after agriculture began in the Fertile Crescent, people poured out of the Middle East, migrating in all directions. Their movement through Europe skirted the mountainous Basque region of the Iberian Peninsula, where an established people apparently resisted intermingling with the newcomers."[2]

The Basques still retain their own tongue. They may seem withdrawn, but really are open-minded. The Basques have an inborn dynamism, sense of justice, devotion to their traditions, and are strong defenders of their cultural identity.

"Let's play honestly, everyone will judge us honorably."

–Basque saying

They are also known for their proverbial agility, *run like a Basque* is a common French saying. They are imaginative, very hospitable and have a deep love for storytelling. The majority of the Basques are thoroughly independent, and are also known for their stubbornness. A nineteenth

---

1   Reprint permission, Time, Inc. from "The Story in Our Genes,"
     TIME magazine, January 16, 1995

2   Reprint permission, *NATIONAL GEOGRAPHIC* from Geographica
     feature: "Mapping Early Migration," September 1994

century English writer described the Basques as being, "Peppery as the Welsh, proud as Lucifer and combustible as his matches."

The complex, precise Basque language, *Euskera* is the oldest known tongue unrelated to any other. Its roots remain, to this day, an enigma. It is an extremely difficult language for outsiders to master, and it is believed by some that Basque was the first human tongue spoken before the Tower of Babel. They are considered the oldest people of Europe, a long surviving race.

In 200 B.C. Romans occupied the Basque region. They were baffled by these people speaking a strange tongue.

A legend states that the devil spent seven years in the Basque Country. To leave he had to cross a bridge. When he arrived on the other side he could only remember, *ez* (no) and *bai* (yes). A way to show that the devil himself could not master the difficult Basque language.

"*Chuchen chuchena dabil Eskualduna* (Straight and upright goes the Basque)."   *–Anonymous*

"*Eskualdun fefedun* (The Basque is faithful)."   *–Proverb*

After 1900, with more than sixty boats, Saint-Jean-de-Luz became the most important European harbor for sardine fishing. As late as the 1930's the town still had a small population of a mysterious race; *Cagots* called *Cascarottes*. The women would sell fish in the streets barefoot, a low basket full of fish on their heads, singing *sardines fraiches* (fresh sardines). In the Middle Ages, *Cascarottes* were considered pariahs or low caste. The Church segregated them from the rest of the congregation and they had their own entrance. Mixed marriages were punishable by death.

A French poet, *Soeur Marie-Ange*, a nun, wrote a short story, "Equinox" about Basque women waiting at the quay in the rain for the return of the fishing fleet. After they safely docked, one fisherman ran toward his fiancee, and taking her in his arms, he murmured in her ear, "*Maita, ene maitia* (Maita, my dearest in the Basque language)." My sister Pauline, the poet used my nickname, a derivative of my given name Marguerite, *Margaita* in Basque. Maita is very close to the verb to love, *maitatu* (I have loved).

For centuries, the Basques have been great seafarers and were the first European whalers. In the sixteenth century, due to the disappearance of whales in the Bay of Biscay, they sailed after their catch as far as Newfoundland and the surrounding areas. They sailed more than 2000 miles, quite a feat! Their skills as navigators, using an intricate system of navigation are legendary. The fishermen would remain west in the New World until they had enough cargo, then return home. Sunken remains of Basque galleons have been discovered in Newfoundland's Red Bay.

In modern times, in Saint-Jean-de-Luz's naturally shel-tered harbor, trawlers painted colorful red, blue or green bobble gently at their moorings following the rhythm of the tides. Depending on the season, the catch is tuna, sardines, anchovies and shell fish. The cannery in the sister city of Ciboure across the river employs more than a thousand local men and women. When the fishing fleet returns to the harbor, the cannery's whistle blows to call the workers. It can be at any time, day or night. In bad weather the foghorns cry plaintively.

Over the centuries, as the sea was encroaching on Saint-Jean-de-Luz, three breakwaters were built following the plans of King Louis XIV's architect, Vauban. These breakwaters seem to encircle the beautiful natural bay in their protective arms; two on each side of the bay connected to land and the third built in the middle of the bay, but not connected to the other two. They are a marvel of engineering, considering the tools available in the seventeenth century. Vauban was also the architect for the fort of Socoa, built to protect the entrance of the bay. All these constructions are still in good shape and are maintained by only a minimum of upkeep.

Breakwater walls in Saint-Jean-de-Luz's bay.

A convent was destroyed by pounding waves, but some stones can still be seen on the beach which was, in 1789, part of the town. It was rebuilt more inland, but at a most inopportune time, the French Revolution had just started.

During the fall equinox the Bay of Biscay has fearsome squalls. Enormous waves pound and leap over the breakwaters. Some of the dying waves reach the beach and the boardwalk, sometimes spraying people watching the spectacular sight.

Saint-Jean-de-Luz's proximity to the Spanish border gave the town strategic importance and also a very interesting history. For the seven centuries prior to the 1940s, in that little corner of the world, Saint-Jean-de-Luz witnessed some major wars. Over the centuries, the kings of France tried to subjugate the Basques, calling them excessively independent, but to no avail. In 732 after conquering Spain, the Moors pushed into Gaul (France) through the Basque region. Abd-el-Rahman's horsemen were stopped in Poitiers by Charles Martel who forced them back over the Pyrénées Mountains into Spain. Martel had checked the further advance of the Moors into Europe. Later the Normans came south. Even in 1152 when Aquitaine was part of the Dominion of England, the Basques retained their independence. During the seventeenth century many wars were fought between France and Spain. After Napoléon appointed his brother Joseph to the vacant throne of Spain, he was unable to quell the patriotic and stubborn Spaniards. Despite all these wars the Basques retained their language and customs.

The roads on the western part of the Pyrénées Mountains have always been well traveled. Over the centuries relay teams of horses were available along the main road from Paris to Madrid. Inns were built adjacent to stables to accommodate travelers arriving in stagecoaches or on foot. Saint-Jean-de-Luz's oldest, Hôtel de la Poste, (hotel for the trading of horses) is still in use after being rebuilt in 1789 and renovated many times. A picture of the hotel adorns the front cover of this book. The hotel has its own fascinating history. If the walls could talk! Later, it was modernized and, in the early thirties, a wing was added by my parents.

The year 1659 placed Saint-Jean-de-Luz on the front page of French history. The Duc de Grammont was selected to ask the hand in marriage of the Infanta, daughter of the King of Spain, for the young, opulent Louis XIV, King of France. May 8, 1660 the King made his grand entrance in Saint-Jean-de-Luz. The wedding took place in the town's old church built in the thirteenth century. As Louis XIV called himself, Sun King, the entrance of the church was walled after the ceremony, never to be crossed again. The following inscription in old French was cut on the exterior of the blocked up door.

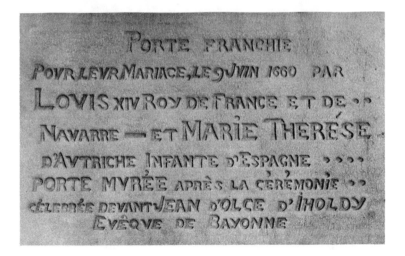

Door crossed for their wedding, June 9, 1660 by King Louis XIV of France, Navarre and Marie Thérèse of Austria, Infanta of Spain. Door bricked up after the ceremony celebrated in the presence of Jean d'Olce d'Iholdy Bishop of Bayonne. (Literal translation by the author)

A week after the wedding, Louis and his new bride left for the Court in Paris. After their departure Saint-Jean-de-Luz was left heavily in debt. Separate buildings, still in use, had been built—one for Louis and another for the Infanta. A very amusing fact is that in 1672 King Louis XIV enacted a law against adultery. The King who had so many mistresses!

In this house which was Hôtel de la Poste of Horses, April 1777 Marquis Marie Joseph Paul de Lafayette received help and assistance on his way to America to take command of the French expeditionary forces. (Literal translation by the author)

In 1777 King Louis XVI of France sent his personal police in pursuit of Lafayette who was on his way to board a ship for America which waited at anchor on the other side of the Pyrénées in Spain. King Louis didn't want him to leave France. Hôtel de la Poste owner's daughter is said to have helped Lafayette hide. A plaque near the hotel's entrance shows a woman with a finger on her lips, warning for silence. (June 25, 1950, Robert Shuman, French Minister of Foreign Affairs came to Saint-Jean-de-Luz for the unveiling ceremony of the commemorative plaque. It drew area dignitaries and naturally, Papa was among them.)

During the twentieth century tourism became the main source of income on the Basque coast. Its temperate climate regulated by the Gulf Stream attracted many vacationers.

In 1875, Maurice Ravel, famous composer of "Bolero," was born in Ciboure across the river from Saint-Jean-de-Luz. The nineteenth and twentieth centuries saw an influx of artists: French writer Pierre Loti, English writer Frances James, and later, Ernest Hemingway; painters Pablo Picasso and Salvador Dali, tenor Enrico Caruso, French singer Edith Piaf and the famous American jazz singer, Josephine Baker. After World War II, Churchill was a frequent visitor to the area.

In winter time, *Luziens* take a breather and go back to their slow pace of living. Many hotels, like my parents', had a regular winter clientele, the English. They loved Saint-Jean-de-Luz's charm, quaintness, slow pace, and balmy winters. Regularly, year after year, many returned to the Hôtel de la Poste away from their country's cold and foggy winters. Some came with their cars and chauffeurs.

Between 1936 and 1939 Saint-Jean-de-Luz was affected by the violent and heinous Spanish Civil War. During thirty-two months, Spain was torn and engulfed in tragic, bloody genocide. Chaos and instability were spreading among the Spanish Basques and Catalans. More than half a million civilians and combatants took refuge in France;

thousands settled in my hometown and surrounding areas. The Spaniards who were too late to escape on the roads were smuggled through the Pyrénées Mountains passes by Spanish Basques.

Hôtel de la Poste, like the other hotels, ran out of room. Mattresses were spread in the hotel hall and sitting rooms. During a school break I had a glimpse of it. It made a lasting impression to see all those people who had to flee their country. They related many tales of horror and atrocities. A Catholic priest, Father Onandia, escaped and was never able to return to Spain. He became a part of our parish.

The border town of Fontarabie was bombed by a single aircraft, which hit only a match factory. The fiery blaze was seen deep across the French border. More refugees poured over the border bridge to the town of Hendaye, filling the already booked hotels to a point beyond saturation.

April 1937, on Good Friday, the defenseless town of Guernica, pride of the Spanish Basque country, was wantonly destroyed by *Luftwaffe* (German Air Force) dive bombers. The town and its inhabitants were crushed under tons of bombs. The Spanish Civil War became a screen for murderous testing of the Reich's latest aircraft and newest arms. Spain's revolution became a training field for German pilots.

Pablo Picasso painted his accusation—the breathtaking painting titled "Guernica." It's described by some historians as a brutally ugly mural, a moral protest against the needless horrors of war. It is said that a German asked Picasso if he had done the painting. His reply was to point toward the canvas answering, "No! You did!"

March 28, 1939 General Franco entered Madrid, ending Spain's bloody, horrendous civil war at the cost of many lives and great suffering. An appropriate quote from Boris Yeltsin perfectly echoes the emotions of that past historical moment, "The flame of civil war has been put out...We have all been scorched by the deadly breath of fratricide..."

In the summer of 1939, vacationers were spending their holidays in Saint-Jean-de-Luz. Hotel rooms were at a premium. Hôtel de la Poste was, as usual, full. In July, my family's four younger children were sent to the country villa deep in the Pyrénées Mountains.

The villa had been built in the early thirties strictly as a summer house. My parents' business didn't give them much time to devote to the care of their younger children. Until I was ten, I was left with a succession of faceless nannies and maids who disappeared without explanations. It left me anchorless. Finally in 1934 a gem was found. *Mademoiselle* Durcudoy, a grammar school teacher, was hired to spend the summers at the villa to supervise the younger Branquet children. A maid-cook would see to the rest of our needs. They were carefree summers with rare visits from my parents. The few times that we went to town in summer, the hotel chauffeur was sent to pick us up. Immediately *Mademoiselle* and I had a special love and bond, which has encompassed sixty years. She became the mother that I had always wished to have. *Mademoiselle* died June 1994, a great loss for me.

My parents belonged to a tenacious, steel-spirited generation which respected effort and discipline. They had traditional principles proving that there is no limit to what people can accomplish if given the opportunity and taking it.

Louis Branquet, my father, five foot five inches tall, had fine features. He was thin and high-strung. He carried himself proudly, was distinguished looking and was always impeccably dressed right down to his fashionable spats. He read widely and possessed an impressive collection of non-fiction books. Papa oversaw the thirty-five employees, which included three chefs. But, he always found time for his favorite sport–hunting.

My mother, Félicie Branquet was a corpulent woman, rather short at about five feet. In her youth, she must have had a different color hair, but I remember only her grey hair streaked with white. She was a gracious and an exceptional business woman. She didn't leave the restaurant food supply shopping to the hotel chef. Twice a week she was seen at the covered market, *les Halles*. She would move from one Basque farm woman's display to another, buying nothing but the best, and also at bargain prices. Produce was weighed on hand scales. Haggling was part of the buying process. Maman would make an offer, automatically the woman said that they could not possibly sell at such a low price. As Maman would walk away, she was immediately called back, "*Madame* Branquet, *huit francs le kilo* (eight francs the kilogram)." The sale was concluded and everyone was happy.

Before I went to boarding school at age ten Maman would sometimes take me with her. Farm women would exclaim, "Is she your daughter, *Madame* Branquet?"

"*Oui*," Maman would reply always addressing them all by their first names, "One of them."

"She is so cute."

Chubby author in baby carriage with Pauline.

Author with Amatxi
(Grandma in Basque).

Pauline, Léon and author in
bathing suits at the beach.

Pauline and author in
their fineries.

Pauline plays nurse
with a reluctant patient.

All of these conversations were in Basque. Maman didn't speak French as a first language and enjoyed every occasion to use her beloved mother tongue. The women who were selling homemade cheese would cut a slice for Maman to taste and naturally a small one for me. It was a real treat!

By their example, my parents tried to instill strong principles of hard work into their seven children hoping that we would follow in their footsteps.

The family was divided into three parts with a twenty-year span between the oldest and the youngest. *Les grands* the three oldest, were Marie, age twenty-nine, chubby and short like Maman; Michel, twenty-seven, stocky and still single; Jeanne, twenty-eight, was thin and sickly, not much was asked of her. Marie and Michel helped my parents at the hotel. *Les petits*, the two youngest, were shy Anne, ten and little devil Marc, nine. Sandwiched in the middle were eighteen-year-old Pauline, and myself, Maita, fifteen. I think that is why both of us have very independent natures. We didn't want to be lost among the other siblings. The four youngest led a peaceful, carefree, very sheltered life, full of comfort.

Despite our opposite personalities and temperament Pauline and I were very close. She was much shorter than I, with dark brown hair, very studious and well behaved. I had much lighter hair, was tall and thin and very energetic. Remarks would often be made by the family, "Is she ever going to stop growing?" until I was as tall as Papa.

Not especially pretty, I had light brown hair which flared with red highlights. As I grew older, the slight curls in my hair disappeared and it turned to a darker brown. I was the only one in the family with hazel-green eyes. I had a vivacious nature, quick to laughter, unable to stay still very long. I had a Leo's sunny personality and was like a butterfly flying from flower to flower, fascinated by life. Tending to look at the brighter side of life. I was nevertheless outgoing only when I was comfortable, then my whole body moved, from arms to hands and legs. My older siblings teased and taunted me; they thought me ungraceful, and clumsy. I was at an awkward age. It was wearisome and their unkind remarks made lasting impressions. As do most Basques, I considered myself Basque first, French second.

Our lives had no equal and many material advantages, but few emotional rewards. At age seven I graduated to eating with my parents, our main meal being at noon time. It was a painful step. Table manners were strictly enforced—no talking, no asking, eat everything on your plate; otherwise, you ate it for supper.

In late August 1939 it was time for the children to leave the country villa after our long summer vacation and go back to the hotel to prepare for the fall school trimester. Uniforms needed to be made ready for the convent boarding school that Pauline and I attended in Pau, eighty miles inland.

When we came home for the Christmas holidays, I could not wait to tell Papa and Maman about our school pilgrimage to the grotto in Lourdes. Our teaching nuns were of the same order that *Sainte Bernadette* had joined after the appearance of the Virgin Mary in that city. During our stay we saw Fred Snite, son of an American millionaire who, due to infantile paralysis, was living in an iron lung.

He was there in the hope of a cure from bathing in the miraculous waters. It was an extraordinary sight.

In our little corner of the world, Pauline and I had been pretty much isolated and living away from the mainstream of events. When we were home at the hotel, which was seldom, we gleaned information at meal time listening to the grownups. We had to listen; children were not allowed into any conversation. Most of it didn't make sense, or rather, I was not much interested in listening to boring adult conversations. I was always anxious for meals to end so I could play.

How could we know that demonic forces were about to sweep Europe? Forces nurtured in the old German Fortress of Landsberg. In 1923 a fanatical political orator, Adolf Hitler, and General Ludendorff tried to organize a coup to overthrow the German Republic. They were unsuccessful in the Beer Hall Putsch, were arrested and sentenced to five years' imprisonment. During his incarceration, Hitler dictated to his faithful friend, Rudolph Hess, chapters of a book later titled, *Mein Kampf* (My Struggles). Its contents were to spew poison through Europe. Hitler was released after serving only nine months of his sentence. His imprisonment was spent in comfort. He had his own room high above the River Lech. Hitler later admitted that without his prison stay *Mein Kampf* would never have been written.

History leaves us the infamous legacy of Hitler's horrendous, murderous, and unbelievable atrocities. His goal—to create a perfect Aryan race, protecting what he thought was the pure German blood. He also wanted to get rid of what he called useless eaters and the imperfect.

Nazi Germany carried out Hitler's *Endlosung* (final solution) which was to kill millions of people: Gypsies, Jews, prisoners of war, dissidents of any kind, by starvation, overwork, disease, torture, slave labor and in gas chambers.

Like a monstrous octopus, his tentacles reached some of the most remote areas of Europe. In June 1940, one of the tentacle's strong grip clenched on a little corner of the world, my hometown, Saint-Jean-de-Luz. As time passed, the Nazi regime turned the tentacles into steel, damaging and destroying millions of lives.

He became a perverter of humanity—including the humanity of the German people and particularly of the German youth.

–Archibald MacLeish, The Eleanor Roosevelt Story

I have often felt bitter sorrow at the thought of the German people, which is so estimable in the individual and so wretched in the generality.

–Goethe

Chapter 1

God gave us brothers. Alas! We invented hate.

–Abbé Gindreau

Unexpected black clouds gathered and were about to burst over Europe.

September 1, 1939–The French mobilized three million men. More than 500 thousand were younger than twenty-five years old. Those soon-to-be soldiers left their jobs, towns, villages and farms. They didn't have the same eagerness as the 1914 First World War soldiers.

France and England declared war against Germany. Neither of the two countries were really ready to face the mighty forces of Hitler's Third Reich. France's armed forces were vastly inferior to the German's, especially her air force and lack of paratroopers.

September 2, 1939–immense, frightening headlines splashed across French newspapers.

C'EST LA GUERRE!..........C'EST LA GUERRE!
IT'S WAR!..........IT'S WAR!

France was at war with Germany! Again. Hitler's Nazi Germany killed the hopes of a peaceful Europe. As in 1914, the war started at the end of the summer.

Posters and newspaper sheets were plastered on kiosks, keeping French people informed. In the thirties it was the primary way of spreading the news.

On September 3, off the coast of Scotland and without warning, the British liner Athenia was torpedoed by a U-30 German submarine. Of the 1400 passengers on board, 112 died, among them thirty-eight Americans. The defenseless ocean liner had been on its way to Canada.

Daily, Papa read the *Le Sud-Ouest*, a newspaper which covered the world news, but especially the events in the southwestern part of France. He had always been abreast of the news and very much interested in politics, but I never knew his political affiliations. I had only heard that my family was blacklisted by the local Communist party.

During the evenings Papa started to glue himself to the TSF, *Télégraphe sans fils* (telegraph without wires, radio), listening to the latest news. The younger children were not allowed to listen to the radio, not even music! Papa often said that the government should have listened to Colonel de Gaulle, who in the thirties had wanted to upgrade the French armed forces. De Gaulle had predicted that more armored divisions and tanks would be needed. After writing several books on the subject, he was brought to the attention of French President Albert Lebrun who didn't believe him. No one had heeded his warnings!

Propaganda from the government on the radio and in the newspapers repeatedly told the nation,

"We will win because we are the strongest!"

After all World War I had been won against Germany. The Third Republic leaders blindly were trying to convince French people that it could easily be done again!

The war revolutionized our peaceful way of living, adding worries about the future, and many uncertainties. Conversations seemed so foreign to what I had previously heard. The words that filtered down to us were fragmented...Hitler...*sales Boches* (dirty Krauts)...war...front. Words rang differently. But there was no sense regretting the music of the past. To me, the war itself seemed so far away and incomprehensible until my brother Michel and my oldest sister Marie's husband Paul were drafted. What a heart wrenching departure! They were leaving to defend our country. The whole family had gathered in our large family/dining room: goodbyes, tears, hugs, nothing made sense. Papa, alone, drove them to the railway station to board trains to their respective assignments.

Soon censored letters arrived from Michel and Paul. They could not divulge their whereabouts. Those were short, laconic letters, most of the time saying, "I am well," only enough to let us know that they were all right.

On September 18, 1939 Pauline turned eighteen. In our culture it was an important milestone. The first trip to Paris, first dance, a gift of a ring or other expensive piece of jewelry. No longer was she forced to eat soup! After meals Pauline would be allowed to drink coffee. In brief, for her it would have been a glimpse of emancipation. The war put a fast stop to these firsts. How weird these allowances of adult freedom seem to me now! But then, at fifteen, many unanswerable questions crowded my mind. Can we ever lead a normal life? If Pauline can't follow customs, how will my teenage years be? What can I look forward to? It felt catastrophic to see them lost. Our normal structured world had come to an abrupt halt, and for how long?

Before the fall classes, some friends and I gave Pauline a costume party. We all left Saint-Jean-de-Luz on our bicycles for the family country villa, taking our costumes with us. Pauline wore the long dress she would have worn for her first ball, which sadly would not happen. I was a *pilotari*, (Basque ball player) dressed in whites, Basque *béret*, *espadrilles*, with the *chistera* (ball game hand basket) tied to my right hand. We had a wonderful time. We didn't know that our first teenagers' party was the last we were going to have for a long time.

Pauline's eighteenth birthday party. Author, front row, first on left; Anne next to her; Pauline, second row, sixth from left.

Early October 1939 Papa drove Pauline and me to the convent high school in Pau which we had been attending. Pau, another city full of history where in the sixteenth century the future king of France, Henry IV, was born. He was made famous in French history by his promise after coronation, "I will put a chicken in every pot of France."

At the convent we were even more shielded from the outside world. Study was still the primary goal, but I tried to do the least that I could. Without trying too hard, I had passing grades. My report cards seemed to be consistent, "Could do better!" Studies were not my favorite subject, recess was! I was intelligent, but never applied myself to school work. I simply wanted to learn what interested me and in my own way. I had a tremendous amount of energy, and definitely made up for disinterest in boring studies with enthusiasm for extracurricular activities. During the day we wore black dresses with blue piping. To go out we had stylish blue uniforms with matching color felt hats. Every weekend we would take walks in columns of two. Often we would see Catholic high school boys doing the same. Shy glances would answer their smiles.

Pauline, cousin Léon and author in their respective high school uniforms.

We had a very stern Mother Superior with piercing eyes. Every Sunday, in the large study hall she conducted for all the pupils a class in manners. On one particular Sunday her topic was hotel and restaurant manners. At one point she stated that when customers didn't eat all their soup, the waiter poured it back into the pot. No sooner had she finished saying the word "pot," than I was up like a jack-in-the-box. Offended, I loudly proclaimed, "*C'est pas vrai* (It's not true)!" I was corrected for interrupting and speaking without permission. But Mother Superior wrote my parents to tell them how fiercely loyal I was to their hotel business.

After hotel food, the convent's bland meals left a lot to be desired. Once a week we ate horse meat. It was supposed to be healthier than other meats! As at home, nothing could be left on our plates. The food was ladled by Sister Marthe who was more than corpulent. Some students, including myself, made derogatory remarks to each other about the possible amount of food she consumed. We ate at long tables. Every student had to bring their own silver place setting, which had to be inscribed with initials and an assigned number. Mine was thirty-eight. Sister Marthe was also mistress of the choir in which Pauline and I sang. We were in charge of distributing and putting away the hymnals.

I felt different from the other boarders as we were probably the only ones who didn't have visits from their parents. The hotel business was too demanding.

In the fall, the nuns brought a poster to the attention of the pupils titled,

SCHOOL, GODMOTHER OF THE SERVICEMAN

It showed a young girl knitting a black sock on a background of the broad blue, white and red bands of the French flag. The caption read: "*Moi aussi avec ma classe, j'ai adopté un soldat* (Me, too! With my class, I have adopted a soldier)."

In my little way, I helped by adopting a nameless soldier, and knitting wool socks for him. Being in a convent school I could not possibly be allowed to correspond with a young man! I hoped that my *chef-d'oeuvre* (masterpiece) would keep his feet warm despite the dreadful colors. It felt good adding my own personal, little contribution.

The nuns launched another war effort—saving paper. Why? The reason is caught in the cobwebs of the past. All students did their homework on a blank sheet of paper in pencil first then over by pen. Both sides were used in the same manner, a lesson which made a lasting impression on me. Half a century later, I use the blank sides of letter size paper for file copies. I am now saving trees. News of the war was brought into the convent by the day students. They sometimes sneaked in newspapers, and we would read the headlines quickly. We didn't want to get caught breaking the rules, punishable by assignment to conjugate verbs during recess. Time I didn't want to waste from having a good time. The nuns really wanted to protect us from the outside world. It was an outstanding private school with high scholarly expectations.

During January 1940, France and Spain signed a trade agreement. Train service which had been interrupted during the three and half years of the Spanish revolution was reinstated between the two countries.

The writing was on the wall. Hitler, who in 1938 had taken Supreme Command of the German Army, was stalling for time. This period was called *La Drôle de Guerre* (The phony war)! There was no offensive from the French. For eight months, the front was immobilized, semi-lethargic, avoiding offensive. A war that France had not wanted, but March, 1939 England and France had pledged their assistance to the Polish Republic.

In the countries that were already occupied by the Germans, invasion, followed by defeat, had been swift and very real. In Holland, Belgium, and Luxembourg, panic and hysteria gripped the people. They didn't know what to do or where to go. An exodus started traveling south, by cars, bicycles, carts, even pushing the sick in baby carriages. Sometimes a bird cage would be seen precariously perched among their meager belongings, cats tied to cords following like dogs. Roads were clogged by the fleeing refugees from three countries and the French from the north. All slowly heading south ahead of the *Wehrmacht*. Millions of Parisians had left the capital. The exodus hampered the French and English military operations.

It was a disastrous campaign for the French. On May 12, 1940 wave after wave of German *Panzerdivisionen* engulfed France from the northwest. In the 1930's, the *Maginot* line had been built to stop an invasion from the Germans. Without forethought from the French military high command and the government, the *Maginot* line ended at the south-eastern Belgian border. France had been slow in extending its defenses as far as the North Sea. It left an open, easily accessible corridor for the *Wehrmacht* to reach France. Invading hordes of German tanks and mechanized infantry, drove around the *Maginot* line. They surged across France like a tidal wave, spilling south—nothing stopped them! In four *stunning* weeks, with speed, strength and ruthlessness, the Germans accomplished what they had not been able to do during the entire four years of World War I.

"The General staff in 1914 was prepared for the war of 1870, and in 1940 for the war of 1914."

–*Guy LaChambre, French Air Minister, 1938-40*

By the end of May, two hundred thousand English and one hundred ten thousand French troops were trapped in northwest France at the port of Dunkirk on the English Channel. In early June, during nine hellish days, the British and French evacuated the troops. Sixty French Navy ships were lost at sea. The evacuation called "Dynamo" was a heroic feat, using at times the smallest private crafts. It was declared the great escape and considered a miracle! After June 4, the remainder of the troops were trapped and taken prisoner by the Germans. Between April and June, 1940 German armies overran six nations.

Letters from Michel and Paul came to an abrupt halt. We were anxious about their whereabouts. Silence! Where could they be? In England? Prisoners? Or dead?

Near Paris gasoline and oil tanks were set afire. Foul-smelling clouds hung over the practically deserted city.

June 13, *Général Henri-Fernand Dentz*, French Military Governor General of Paris, declared Paris, "*Ville Ouverte* (Open City)" asking Parisians to abstain from hostile acts and conduct themselves with composure and dignity. Paris had been abandoned by its leaders and the French Army.

Parisians assailed railway stations, left by car, or any way they could. Outside the city their numbers were increased by farmers, pushing carts and taking their cattle with them. They were following the massive exodus. Out of a population of approximately three million fewer than a third stayed. Oppressive silence hung over Paris. By nightfall, the *Wehrmacht*, in waves of *verdigris* (a poisonous shade of bluish-green), marched into what had become virtually a ghost town. Immediately, Nazi red flags with their offensive *swastikas* (design of ancient origin, a bent-arm cross, which the Germans used as the Nazi party emblem and symbol of anti-Semitism) appeared on buildings, and on the pride of Parisians, the Eiffel Tower. France was defeated and disgraced.

The French Government abandoned Paris, straggling south to Bordeaux. Between the Government and the refugees, that city's population swelled from two hundred eighty thousand to eight hundred thousand. Because Saint-Jean-de-Luz was so far from Paris, and 200 kilometers from Bordeaux, the exodus didn't reach our area.

The following day, the French Government was in Bordeaux. Two days later, Paul Reynaud resigned as premier and the cabinet fell. It was a crucial week-end! June twenty-fifth he was replaced by eighty-four year old Field Marshal Henri Pétain who asked the next day for an armistice. He set up a collaborationist French government in Vichy. With a senile voice he addressed the nation on radio asking the troops to stop fighting and to put their arms down. "*Français* (Frenchmen)! Following the request of the President of the Republic, I am assuming the helm of the Government of France...I give France the gift of my person!"

Pierre Laval was elected Vice-President and took control of the press and radio.

France's Third Republic had lived its last days!

In northeast France, Alsace-Lorraine was again declared German territory. Since 1870 it had changed hands three times: 1870-1918 German, 1918-1940 French. The Rhine River, making a natural border between France and Germany situated Alsace-Lorraine on the French side of the river. Unwillingly, generation to generation changed nationality. Despite that fact most of them stayed, their roots were ingrained in that corner of the world.

The BBC, British Broadcasting Co., started regular broadcasts in French. In July Charles de Gaulle sent a message from London to his countrymen, "The fighting is not ended!"

Now the younger Branquet children heard different words trickling down to them...troops fought with bravery and tenacity...resigned...Pétain...traitor...lies...armistice...disaster. Like the whole family, I also felt deeply the shame of our defeat.

After only ten months of the *drôle de guerre* (phony war), a crushing defeat. The 1918 illusion of victory had been followed by a peculiar peace of twenty-two years. World War II would depose Europe from its old position of world dominance.

After the Germans' victory of 1940, one hundred thousand French and civilians were dead. More than a million and a half French soldiers were in German hands. They were deported to various prison camps as virtual hostages of the Third Reich.

Some became slave laborers, forced to work in factories
and on farms. The prisoners were on a starvation diet,
suffered from the cold, their clothes in shreds. The proximity of overcrowded barracks, the bugs, shortages of food
and at times water, were often unbearable. Tempers flared.
How they looked forward to receiving parcels and letters
from home. Still, by the end of July, two hundred fifty
thousand had either been released or had escaped.

"Victory...defeat...words without meaning. A victory
weakens one nation, a defeat arouses another."

                            –*Antoine de Saint-Exupery, Night Flight*

June 22, 1940

La Guerre est terminée
The war is ended

Deuil national (National mourning)
Armistice effective Tuesday, June 25
Signatures were exchanged last night at 18:35
Cease fire this morning at 01:35
CANNONS ARE SILENT
"It will be many years before the stain of 1940 can be
effaced...it was the most shocking collapse in all the history
of our national life..."

                  –*Marc Bloch, before his execution by the Nazis in 1944*

In 1525, French King *François Ier* (Francis, the First)
said after losing a battle, "All has been lost save honor."
In 1940 France's honor was lost! The country had
sunk in quicksand, the French felt disgraced. Humiliating
surrender!

The armistice conditions were very harsh, swiftly enforced and devastating. One was the payment of nine million dollars a day for compensation, thus the occupied were forced to pay for their occupier's upkeep! The French army was reduced to a remnant of one hundred thousand. The Press would be controlled by the Nazis and industries were forced to start manufacturing for the Third Reich. Each week, cattle, butter and other supplies were requisitioned then shipped to Germany.

Three-fifths of France was going to be occupied, which would be in the best interests of the Third Reich. It gave Germany complete control of France's Atlantic coast and access to Spain. France would be divided like two foreign countries, separated across thousands of miles by an ill-defined demarcation line.

WE WERE GOING TO BE PRISONERS
IN OUR OWN COUNTRY!

In the occupied zone, the French administration ceased to exist and was replaced by Nazi rule.

Many years before the war, Germany had planted spies in French industries and major administrations. They had also recruited French men and women who were sympathetic to the Nazi cause. These people were called the Fifth Column helping the Germans by reporting valuable information on France's military strength. What infamy!

As soon as the news that France was to be divided spread to our high school boarding convent, Mother Superior called an emergency meeting of the nuns. No sooner was that meeting over than the nuns scurried around the school corridors, their veils flying behind them like birds of darkness. Classes were interrupted, *"Vite, vite, dépéchez-*

vous, mes enfants (Hurry, hurry, be quick, my children)!"
All the students were instructed to immediately go to
assembly hall.

The students could not imagine what was going on. In
the past three years we had never seen the nuns in such a
state. Pauline and I found each other running toward the
hall. Like the other students, we settled quietly. Silently we
looked at each other, shrugging our shoulders in a questioning
manner. Most of the other students were whispering.

When Mother Superior arrived at the door, as was
customary, all the students got up. Complete silence in the
room! We had noticed how solemn she was.

"Children, sit down. I have some very bad news."

Pauline and I looked at each other, puzzled.

Mother Superior continued, "As German troops are
coming south rapidly, we are closing the school." We all
gasped, looking at each other in disbelief as she continued,
"They will be here soon. France is going to be divided. I
want all the students who are going to be living in the
occupied zone to leave immediately. You need to arrive at
your homes before the Germans. When I call your name,
hurry, go pack your clothes. Do not take your school books.
It would be too much to carry. As soon as you are finished,
rush to the front entrance. You are all going to be taken to
the railway station to catch the first available trains to your
hometowns. Your parents have been notified. Students
who have not been called, go immediately to the recreation
room, and PLEASE stay out of the way." From Mother
Superior we had never before heard such a tone, nor such
orders. Softly, she added, "*Que Dieu vous bénisse* (May God
bless you)!"

Pauline and I followed her instructions. We rushed upstairs to the dormitory. In no time we were packed and at the front door ready to be driven to the railway station. On the train we were so stunned that even I remained silent. We sat gloomily facing each other. The clicking and pounding of the wheels repeated in my head, the Germans are coming, the Germans are coming! The Germans are coming! Was I ever going to see the landscape between Pau and home again? Would we be able to go back to school? Would we arrive home ahead of the soldiers? Questions, questions tumbled in my mind.

When we arrived in Saint-Jean-de-Luz, Papa was waiting for us at the railway station. The short ride to the hotel was made in total silence. At home there was an air of sadness, like a veil of gloom. At that time our future looked very bleak, uncertain and scary.

On June 22, as dawn was beginning to break, the Chief of Police and several *gendarmes* (policemen) arrived at the hotel door, pounding, using their whistles to arouse us. Papa was the first at the entrance.

"*Monsieur* Branquet," said the chief, "several English ships are anchored in the bay. Round up all your English clients. They are being evacuated to England. Only one suitcase per person can be taken. They must be at the pier no later than six. Launches will be available to transport them from the pier to the ships."

Immediately, Papa woke the whole family giving each one of us specific instructions. We dressed in a hurry, ran through the hotel corridors, screaming and pounding indiscriminately on all the bedroom doors. We didn't have time to check whether the rooms were occupied by English clients. Sleepy heads appeared at the doors.

"What is it?" puzzled they asked.

Other hurried questions would follow, but we could only ask, "Are you English?" If the answer was yes, the few family members who, like me, could speak some English, would give instructions.

"Hurry up, the Germans are coming south fast. A ship is waiting in the harbor to evacuate you to England. You can only take one suitcase, hurry downstairs. Papa or the chauffeur will drive you to the pier." It was sheer panic and pandemonium. Nobody bothered to see if the hotel chauffeur was wearing his uniform and cap. Papa drove some of them in the family car.

A spinster, Miss Oding, had been a client of the hotel for more than fifteen years. As no one had seen her, Papa dispatched me to her second floor bedroom. Pounding on her door, I was unable to arouse her. We all knew that she was very fond of her cognac. My only recourse was to run downstairs to get the duplicate key. Corridors, stairs, and the entryway were bedlam. With difficulty I was able again to reach her room. Opening the door, I found Miss Oding sound asleep, snoring loudly. It was quite a job waking her. Opening her eyes, she groggily asked in French, with her delightful clipped British accent, "Oh! Maita! *Que faites-vous dans ma chambre* (What are you doing in my room)?" Had it been another time, it would have been comical.

As fast as I could, in my very accented high school English I explained the situation, helped her dress, pack, and walked her downstairs. After the war she came back and died at the hotel. We were her only family.

Her fondness for cognac had at times created some hilarious incidents, for example, one day she majestically walked down the large hotel stairs wearing an open rain-coat—that's all!

As they left, the panic-stricken English clients asked my parents to take care of their remaining belongings.

The vessel, Batory, left last, taking remnants of the Polish army which had trickled south, some French soldiers, and student pilots from a nearby French Air Force base. These English ships were the last ones to drop anchor in Saint-Jean-de-Luz's bay until 1944. The weather cooperated with a very calm sea.

After the departure of the English clients, we were all exhausted. Papa and Maman sent us back to bed for a couple hours of sleep. Still more work had to be done. Early the following morning we went to their rooms to pack their belongings. But, what to do with them? They needed to be hidden before the arrival of the Germans. Papa came up with the most brilliant idea of piling the suitcases in a large, windowless bathroom. The door was removed, a wall installed, plastered, painted, and a sink installed in front of the former door. Fast work! No one would be able to tell except us!

The *Wehrmacht* moved swiftly toward the southwest. On the twenty-seventh, Saint-Jean-de-Luz was one of the last French cities to be occupied, being 700 kilometers from Paris. The Basque region was occupied without a shot being fired.

A cloud of soberness hung over our family. Again and again I asked myself, "What is going to happen to us?"

Putting events and emotions into words made things more understandable, less overwhelming.
    –Claire McCarthy, MD, Learning How the Heart Beats

Chapter 2

A clever conqueror will always, if possible, impose his demands on the conquered by installments.

–Adolf Hitler

On June 26, the mayor of Saint-Jean-de-Luz received a call from his counterpart in Bayonne (good river in Basque), a large city twenty kilometers north. He was to alert the *Luziens* that the Germans would arrive the following day.

In 1940 telephone subscribers were not plentiful except businesses, they called each other with the sad news. Each one of them was to contact as many neighbors as possible. People knocked at each others' doors, spreading the tragic news like wildfire. A heavy cloud of impending danger fell over my hometown.

The following day *Le Sud-Ouest* had sad, bold-lettered headlines quoting General Lafont, Commandant of the 18th Region:

"Frenchmen, have dignity! Don't be curious bystanders looking at the parade of foreign troops on our soil. Be correct, close your windows."

Saint-Jean-de-Luz seemed asleep; house windows and shutters were closed. Businesses had turned their signs to *Fermé* (Closed). Streets and sidewalks were deserted as a show of protest. Dogs and cats were kept indoors. NO sign of life!

The *Wehrmacht* was expected to arrive down National 10, the road which passes in front of the Hôtel de la Poste. They would enter a seemingly abandoned city.

June 18, mid-afternoon, DEATHWATCH SILENCE.

Suddenly a strange low rumbling noise like drums could be heard in the distance. It became louder and louder. It was the harsh sound of armored cars, sidecars painted a depressing *verdigris*. They were followed by a perfect formation of tall, fair, healthy looking, stiff Teuton foot soldiers, immaculately dressed in uniforms and helmets of that same sickening color. Wave after wave of them, red flags with the detested swastika flapping in the wind, their highly polished, black hobnailed boots hitting the pavement in unison with a deafening beat. This sea of drab color was a shocking contrast to our colorful Basque town of white houses with bright green or red shutters and red-tiled roofs.

From a second floor hotel window, behind latticed shutters, I peeked. My younger sister, Anne, age ten, a cute little girl with fringed black bangs tugged at my sleeve and whispered, "*Maita, qu'es que c'est* (what is it)?"

She was not tall enough to see through the shutters. I felt her little trembling hand grab mine. What could I tell her?

"*C'est les Boches qui arrivent* (The Krauts are arriving)!" At her age it didn't mean much, but still it was for both of us a scary moment.

Hôtel de la Poste on Rue Gambetta (renovated). Ground floor first two windows to the right were the Branquet family living/dining room. From behind closed shutters on the second floor author and little sister Anne watched the German troops' arrival in Saint-Jean-de-Luz.

The sea of ugly green passed in front of the hotel. The light-skinned soldiers marched with fixed stares, looking straight ahead. Their blaring singing in that guttural tongue was offensive to our Latin ears. I didn't want to look anymore.

"*Partons* (Let's go)," I told Anne walking away from the window. We could not stay behind those shutters forever. Despite the Germans' arrival, the world would still be out there, sunshine, the beach. They would not disappear! We were alive!

Again, I was asking myself, what kind of a life are we going to lead? Millions of questions nibbled at my young mind. What is going to happen to all of us? Would we be able to spend this summer at the country villa at the foot of the Pyrénées? The marching soldiers were a difficult sight for two young people who had lived until now in a protected environment, enjoyable and worry free. Until later, I was unaware that June 27, 1940 was the start of many years which were going to drastically change the course of our family's life and especially mine. I was soon going to turn sixteen years old. My teenage formative years would be *stolen*.

OUR WORLD WOULD NEVER BE THE SAME.
NEVER AGAIN!

Twenty kilometers south that same day, the *Wehrmacht* reached Hendaye. Now France was occupied to the Spanish border.

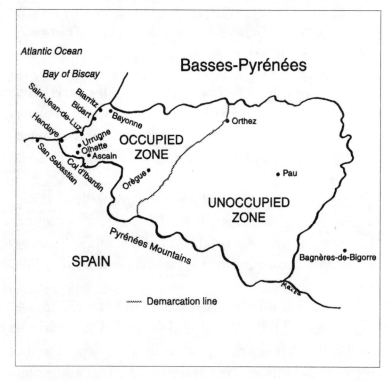

Map of Basque region

Right away, all strategic towns would have a *Komman-dantur* (German headquarters) located in a requisitioned hotel, which housed a *Kommandant* (high ranking German officer) and his staff.

On Thursday, June 28, the *Kommandant* of Saint-Jean-de-Luz had posters plastered on kiosks and building walls all over the city. The same message appeared in *Le Sud-Ouest*.

THE ONES WHO ACT CALMLY AND PEACEFULLY HAVE NOTHING TO FEAR

Soon after, another poster appeared,

ABANDONED FRENCH PEOPLE, TRUST THE GERMAN SOLDIERS

It showed the picture of a smiling German soldier holding in his arms a French child. A French journalist called the poster, "A calm and tidy rape, overwhelming the French people."

Strict orders had been given by the High German Command to the occupation forces. They were to do their best to charm the French and to behave correctly and courteously. To the point of opening doors for women. Nazi Germany needed to keep the French economy producing at full capacity. Farmers' produce was essential to feed the Third Reich population and armed forces.

The German officers strongly discouraged the soldiers from having sexual relations with French women—a command which was going to be to our advantage. The veiled warning meant, "They are all diseased!" The German soldiers were ordered not to talk to strangers, their superiors being afraid that they would divulge military secrets.

First edict: Curfew from 2100 (9 p.m.) until 0530 (5:30 a.m.) with strict adherence to blackout. Heavy fines by the Germans were extracted for non-compliance. That edict would be followed by many other orders complicating our simple lives.

Other posters with a print date of May 10 showed how well-prepared, organized, and sure of their victory the Third Reich had been.

POSSESSIONS OF ARMS
IN THE OCCUPIED ZONE

Within twenty-four hours, all arms, grenades, and explosives have to be deposited with French authorities at *Hôtel de Villes* (Town Halls). Death penalty for non-compliance. Acts of violence against members of the *Wehrmacht* will be punishable by death. Lesser infractions will be punishable by imprisonment.

Saint-Jean-de-Luz was inundated by posters, but as in Paris, they were often torn down as fast as they were pasted up.

The two words, "German soldier" were immediately replaced by the term *Boche* (Kraut). It originated from the shortened French word *caboche*, meaning of hard head or a stupid man. An epithet now always used as an insult. Everything bad was added to this attribute, "You are like a *Boche*." "You lie like a *Boche*." "You are dumb like a *Boche*." The list was endless.

In our streets, the tall, mostly blond Germans walked in such a different way, stiffly, some very clumsily. Their officers had an air of superiority and arrogance.

My former middle school teacher, *Mademoiselle* Durcudoy, now ninety-two years old, recalls those days:

"As soon as the *Kommandant* arrived in the Basque region, he gave the order that schools had to immediately close their doors. They were to remain closed until he gave the order to reopen them.

"Superintendents of public schools decided to start the summer vacation early. In Hendaye where I taught at a private school, the headmistress, *Mademoiselle* Suertegaray, despite their edict, continued classes. One was conducted in the covered playground, another in a neighbor's garage and the third in the director's home. They proceeded that way until the end of the school year in July. It was very brave of her to defy the Germans' orders.

"Another immediate order was that clocks be moved to German time! It was still dark when the classes started. Thursdays were a half day of school. In the afternoon students enjoyed long strolls, two by two, supervised by a teacher. One day the students were famished. I stopped at a bakery to buy some bread, but my request was turned down. It was the beginning of problems with many store owners who were starting to hoard food."

Pauline and I had attended that school as boarders for three years, from 1934 to 1937. When enrolled I was only ten years of age, very young. During those years with the help of my tutor, *Mademoiselle* Durcudoy, I was a straight A student.

VERBOTEN (forbidden)

A word which was going to haunt us for years. We would often ask ourselves, what is not forbidden by the Germans?

June 28, 1940

Ban of all movement/travel between the two French zones, occupied and unoccupied Vichy-France.

The demarcation line was declared impassable by the Germans without an *Ausweis* (Permit). It was a very erratic line; barriers could be found on roads, in the middle of fields, and at times even cutting villages in two. Signs were posted.

Demarkationslinie uberschreiten verboten
(Demarcation line, forbidden to pass)

The occupied zone guaranteed the Germans control of the Atlantic coast, and a land link with Spain through a small portion of the western Pyrénées Mountains which included part of the Basque region.

France had eighty-two *départments* (similar to states in the U.S.). Saint-Jean-de-Luz was located in the department of *Basses-Pyrénées*, (low Pyrénées) now divided in two by the demarcation line.

Immediately, *Kommandanturs* received an onslaught of *Ausweis* requests. Separated families wanted to see each other, celebrate marriages, baptisms and comfort each other when a death occurred. Business transactions were interrupted. All sorts of tricks and reasons were used on the applications, especially serious sickness or death in a family. Very few were granted. When denied, it left only one recourse—sneak through. The demarcation line gave birth to a brisk business of ferrying people through illegally. Some dishonest smugglers charged exorbitant fees to help people cross to the unoccupied zone.

Opposite of the obedient, regimented Germans, the French, especially the Basques, enjoyed breaking rules, and especially the multitude of edicts imposed by the Third Reich.

THE PRISON WALLS ARE CLOSING TIGHT!

So the Germans thought!

"Though a good deal is too strange to be believed, nothing is too strange to have happened."

—Thomas Hardy

In early July, Field Marshal Pétain's new government moved to the spa-town of Vichy in central unoccupied France. He continued his adopted policy of collaboration with the enemy, the Nazis. By allowing Pétain's puppet regime, Hitler was advising the world that Vichy had joined him against England. Still Vichy-France refused Hitler's request for the use of French Military bases in Africa, probably their only act of considerable courage. Parliament voted itself out of existence, giving Pétain dictatorial power. He became a sort of old dictator trying to copy some aspects of the Nazi regime. The *Führer's* scheme toward France in the long run helped ruin him.

Because the large Branquet family had a vast difference of age between the oldest and the youngest children, twenty years, the German occupation was going to affect us differently. The three oldest had their careers, *les petits* were too young. Three years older than I, Pauline already knew what she wanted to do with her life. After graduation she would join the Sisters of Charity of Nevers, the same order as our high school nuns.

My teenage years were going to be lived under the German occupation. I was going to be robbed of those good formative and fun years by the upheavals of war and those *sales Boches* (dirty Krauts). Gone was the first trip to Paris, new clothes instead of my oldest sister Marie's hand-me-downs. Gone were glimpses of independence.

That summer Maman, realizing that our lives were rather grim, gave Pauline and me money to spend the afternoon in Bayonne. What a treat! Until then pocket money had been non-existent. All excited, we boarded the train. In the thirties it had been fashionable to go to tea shops for hot chocolate or tea and pastries. We went to Dodin, the most expensive tea shop in town. With relish we stuffed ourselves with delicious French pastries which were soon to disappear for lack of staples.

Leaving Dodin, feeling very grown up, we went shopping which we never had done alone. It was so exciting going from store to store and looking leisurely at shop windows, not having an adult to tell us what to do. In a department store we saw some shiny earrings. As we still had some money left, we decided to buy two pairs. How beautiful they were! What a good time we were having, we didn't want to go home. But it was no time to push our luck! On the way home from the railway station in Saint-Jean-de-Luz, we could not wait to show our oldest sister Marie our purchases. We were so proud of the colorful earrings we had bought by ourselves. Marie found them cheap and dreadfully gaudy! She forbade us to wear them.

She was, of course, right but she burst our bubble of happiness.

In the fall, Marie received notification that her husband Paul was a prisoner of war. She was devastated, but he was alive! How could she explain to her little daughters that she didn't know when their Papa would come home? Maman tried to comfort her the best she could.

Not a word from my brother Michel, where could he be? Prisoner? Missing? Dead? or in England? My parents didn't want to show their deep worries about his whereabouts.

Our sadness was intensified by the death of our twenty-nine-year-old sister, Jeanne. She had always been sickly, but ever so talented. Jeanne had taken piano lessons from our world renowned church organist, *Monsieur* Lebout. She became an accomplished pianist. When I was little, I would dance and dance behind her while she played the piano. Due to our difference in age, thirteen years, and time away from home, I never had the chance to know her well and it added to my sense of loss.

In our culture, her medical condition was never discussed, as a consequence we didn't ask the cause of her death. Had her disorder been accepted and discussed openly she might not have committed suicide. Jeanne had psychomotor epilepsy, a disorder which until this day is misunderstood and carries a strong social stigma. The lack of openness from my parents influenced me greatly and negatively when at age forty-four I developed nocturnal epilepsy after a horrible head trauma. In 1993, my goal to help people with the disorder and those who have survived a violent crime took form in my book, *Don't shoot! My life is valuable.*

Rations became another unpleasant plural word added
to our vocabulary. It meant that food would be taken away
from our mouths to feed the Germans. First to be rationed
were bread, milk, rice, pasta, and, of all things—soap.
Ration cards had different categories, mine was J3 issued
for ages thirteen to twenty-one.

We could not stand to see the soldiers buying everything
they wanted, paying for their multitude of purchases with
brand new *Francs* at a rate of exchange disgustingly advan-
tageous for them. Like tourists, they bought souvenirs,
emptying our favorite stores of their contents. Everyday
Papa complained vehemently of this plundering, "Those
pigs are taking everything!"

Summertime in Saint-Jean-de-Luz, *fiacres* (horse drawn
carriages) had always been fashionable for transportation
within the city. Beginning in summer 1940, as gas was
becoming more difficult to obtain, *fiacre* driving became a
year-round lucrative job. They became taxi substitutes along
with the *vélo-taxis*. These looked like rickshaws, but instead
of the man running, he was on a bicycle. In our area the
drivers wore Basque *bérets*, white rolled up sleeve shirts,
and sandals. More often than not, a cigarette dangled from
the corner of their mouths. *Le Sud-Ouest* showed pictures
of taxis in Paris, old cars sawed in two, drawn by a horse.
The French were using their imaginations.

Slowly cars disappeared from the roads. Because one of
my uncles owned a garage near the hotel, Papa's supply of
gasoline lasted longer than the average *Luzien's*. Soon
bizarre looking converted cars, called *gazogènes* (gas producing) appeared on the nearly deserted roads. They were
propelled by charcoal or wood burned in contraptions

which looked like water heaters made of metal bolted to the trunks. They were quite a feat of ingenuity, and they worked! The combustion went directly to the carburetors. What a weird sight on the roads, and on the shoulders when their drivers stoked their boilers leaving behind piles of ashes. Within several months, in the occupied zone, deaths due to car accidents became practically a thing of the past. Only three deaths were reported until the end of the year. As a mode of transportation, horses and buggies came third in line, back to the old days!

Bicycles took the place of honor on the roads. From June until the end of the year, ten million bicycles were sold!

Pauline and I were quite a feisty pair possessed with demons of imagination which often got us in trouble, mostly with Papa. We had devised a coded language only known to us. The *Boches* were labeled *haricots verts* (green beans), the color of their uniforms and we had our little antics at their expense. Any man in our summer resort town of twelve thousand who was unknown to us, was declared suspicious, especially if he wore a black leather coat, felt hat, and boots. We would follow these men in the streets to see where they were going. When Papa heard of our efforts to save the country, he harshly scolded us.

"*Vous êtes folles* (You are crazy)! What am I going to do with you two? Those men are the dreaded Gestapo who dress that way. The Gestapo drive black Citroen 11 CV. When you see them it only means *trouble*. They just requisitioned the Pension Lillia behind the hotel. It will be their Headquarters. You are going to get all of us into trouble!"

Papa managed to scare us. His anger at us was well deserved, for taking such risks. Until then we had no idea what the Gestapo was. In our little corner of the world, they were not often seen openly. But the Gestapo's monstrous reputation was very real.

One boring summer day in the hotel hall, Pauline and I saw a man fitting our overworked imaginations' description of a spy. In our estimation, he looked out of place. And to top it all, he was hiding behind a newspaper. Boldly we walked toward him. Pauline, being the oldest, approached him. I was her sidekick and moral support.

"What do you wish, Sir?" she was more than brave to ask.

With a rustle, *Le Sud-Ouest* newspaper came down. A middle aged, silver-haired man with a large walrus mustache whipped off his reading glasses, looked up at us scornfully.

"And what do you want, young ladies?" he gruffly demanded.

We were caught at our own game. Pauline could not think of an answer. We made a hasty retreat, realizing that he was a hotel client who didn't appreciate our snooping around.

To ward off possible advances from the soldiers, we learned a few German words, *Nicht spagen sie deutsche* (I don't speak German). It was enough! They never persisted as they were very disciplined. Passing by women in the streets, their comments were uniform, no variation or originality! "*Oh! la, la, Matemoiselle,*" they would all say. With their heavy accent the *d* in *Mademoiselle* sounded like a *t*. When this happened to us, automatically our heads would turn away and often, we would make an about face to walk in the opposite direction.

We often played a game on main street. Most French town have a *rue* (street) named after the last century's famous French orator *Léon Gambetta*. Due to our town centuries' old origin, the sidewalks are narrow enough to accommodate only one person at a time. *Luziens*, being very independent and not inclined to discipline, usually walked in the middle of the street, especially since by then few cars were seen around town, and those were German. Whenever Pauline and I would see a soldier walking in the opposite direction on a sidewalk, as well disciplined Germans would do, one of us would say, *haricots verts*.

Mutual complicity emerged from our movements. We would then rush to the side of the street where they were walking, glue our noses to a store window, looking very much interested in its display, even if it was the hardware store. By doing so, the soldiers had to step down into the street around us. Hurrah! We made them give way! Pauline and I kept count of all our private victories. Besides being feisty, Pauline and I were the most independent and adventurous of the Branquet children.

High ranking German officers' summer uniform jackets were white! They looked to us like waiters. Walking down our main street, *rue Gambetta* passing by them, Pauline and I would take turns saying loudly, "*Garçon, deux bocks* (Waiter, two beers)!"

We were mocking their uniforms. Dangerous? Who knows! They probably didn't pay attention to us and few understood French. But, oh! what fun!

Another ban was the display of French flags. We had some very small ones on our bicycles. These petty German edicts didn't phase us a bit. It seemed that their language when speaking to the French was merely made of ONE word, *VERBOTEN*. That word was an incentive for us, and most French people, to do the opposite. Another word soon was heard, *ACHTUNG* (attention)! To me it sounded like a sneeze. We would say, "God bless you!" How we giggled!

Pauline had an unusual brooch with three swallows and the inscription, "They will return," meaning only to us, the prisoners of war. One day as we were walking and talking about it on main street, an officer of average height with broad shoulders and piercing blue eyes stopped us. Pointing to the brooch he brusquely asked, "*Quoi* (what)?"

Very calmly Pauline improvised an answer, "The swallows return every year." Close call? Really, what could they do? Put us all in jail? They had more pressing problems than dealing with French young people.

One unreasonably hot and sunny day, Maman called Pauline. "Set a table in the employees' dining-room for a German soldier. He came in the hotel with a fish that he has caught and asked if the chef could cook it."

Pauline refused, "I can't do that!"

"You must," answered Maman, "he was polite and we must be gracious."

Pauline always remembered that powerful lesson in basic human manners.

Still no news from Michel. Daily, my cute, dainty little sister Anne would be on the lookout for the arrival of the old mailman, Emile, whom she loved. He was replacing our regular mailman who had been mobilized and was a prisoner of war. Emile's appearance was the highlight of her day. Taking the mail from him gave her a sense of importance. Emile had a weathered face, soft brown eyes and a constant smile. He would lumber up our street pushing his old bicycle. In late July he gave her a postcard. Her little legs danced until she found Papa. As usual, he was sitting in his favorite chair, reading.

"Papa, Papa, *du courrier* (mail)," she breathlessly said.

As he heard her pretty little voice, he put his book down. Looking up smiling, he asked, "What did old Emile give you today?"

"A pretty postcard," she answered, waving it.

After reading a few lines an excited Papa jumped out of his chair. "But, it's Michel's handwriting. Anne, hurry, hurry! Run, go find Maman."

She soon came back with Maman following her who, out of breath, asked, "But, Louis what's going on? What is so important?"

"A card from Michel."

"A card from Michel! It is not possible!" Maman exclaimed. After taking the card in her trembling hands she pressed it to her heart. Maman could only whisper, "*Merci, Mon Dieu* (Thank you, God)!"

At dinner time Papa warned all of us, "This has to be kept quiet. NO ONE must know, and, Maita, you absolutely can't even tell your cousin Léon." It would be hard for me because since the occupation we had become inseparable. Oh, well, I thought, keeping a secret is living in danger. That was exciting.

The card was signed Michelle, the feminine of Michel. My brother Michel had been careful and imaginative because mail was censored. The card being postmarked

Paris, my parents felt that he was all right. A couple of days later, Emile gave Anne another postcard. It was from "Michelle" again. The card stated that "she" was very tired and that the doctor had prescribed a long rest near the seashore! She would arrive by train real soon...How clever of our brother!

After receiving the second postcard, *Mademoiselle* Durcudoy, our teacher/governess who was staying with us at the hotel, Pauline and I diligently went daily to the railway station to meet the train from Paris. Each time we had to buy special access tickets allowing us to wait on the platform. Several times we saw an elderly couple also waiting. Were they waiting for their son? How many times did we go to the railway station ten minutes walk from the hotel? It is lost in the cobwebs of my mind.

One day, a man whose premature balding made him look older than his age, stepped down from a compartment. He put a finger on his lips. Papa had warned us not to make any sign of knowing who Michel was. As the man approached us, I noticed that he was so skinny. He looked so much like Michel. It was him! It was so hard not to run and hug him. At the exit, Michel was walking behind me to surrender his train ticket as is customary at French railroad stations. After I gave my platform access ticket to the ruddy faced railroad employee, I heard him say to Michel as he was passing through, "I had heard that you were a prisoner of war."

Nonchalantly, Michel answered, "What makes you think that? I was visiting relatives in Paris."

We waited until we were no longer within sight of the railway station to talk to Michel. While walking back to the hotel I could not contain my impatience. Excitedly, I asked him endless questions.

"Be patient," Michel scolded, "wait until we get home, then I will tell my story."

The wait was longer than I thought, until after dinner when the whole family was gathered together. Michel recounted his incredible escape story. I hung onto his every word.

"I had indeed been taken prisoner in northern France. With other French prisoners I was being marched toward Germany. Soldiers guarding us on either side. As an officer I had fought the war in a motorcycle sidecar, my feet were not used to long forced marches. Very fast I developed immense blisters which started to bleed. I could not take another step, and just fell on the side of the road, not caring what would happen to me. A gruff, enormous German soldier with wire-rimmed glasses came toward me. I showed him my feet. He gestured to wait. With sign language and pidgin French he told me that a truck was picking up stragglers. Eventually, I found myself alone! Why not escape? How would the Germans ever find out that one French officer was missing? Suddenly, I didn't care how badly my feet would bleed. I hid in a nearby field behind a haystack. Exhausted, I immediately fell asleep. Next morning, very early I woke up with a start, a noise. I looked up. Facing me was an old, graying farmer, his tanned face carved with lines. He pointed his pitchfork at me. My first thought was, that's it! He is going to turn me over to the Germans. I decided to gamble and cried out, 'I am an escaped prisoner! Please help!' When the farmer, smilingly extended his hand, I knew that I was temporarily saved.

"Pierre the farmer took me to his farmhouse. His plump, rosy-cheeked wife fed me the best meal I'd had since the start of the war. Later they hid me in the loft. Still exhausted and well fed I instantly fell asleep. As soon as my feet healed, Pierre got in touch with an underground network which had already started to help escaped prisoners. His first instructions were that I not shave. He gave me some old clothes as he had burnt my uniform with the garbage. I really looked like a tramp especially with the unkempt beard. Pierre gave me food, some money and a map to Paris supplied by the underground. What an exhausting and scary trip.

"Surprisingly, on the road no one paid attention to me. As soon as I arrived in Paris, I took the metro (subway) to Papa's cousin Olga's apartment. I knocked softly. When she opened the door, as I looked so bad, Olga didn't recognize me and was about to scream. I quickly put my finger on my lips whispering, 'It's me, Michel.' I started to cry from sheer exhaustion and stress. It was so good seeing a family member.

"My presence forced Olga to do her grocery shopping at night and at distant stores, not wanting anyone to inquire why all of a sudden her purchases were too much for one person. One never knew whether an informer might be among her neighbors or be the grocery store owner. If I were found in her apartment, both of us would have been arrested and our lives would have been in great danger. Especially Olga's for harboring an escaped prisoner. She would have been shipped to a concentration camp in a cattle car, and I would have been sent to a prisoner of war camp in Germany." What a saga!

After Michel's return, Papa and Maman were always worried because he was so stupidly reckless. Once a week, Pauline and Michel went to the movies. I was considered by Maman too young to join them. It didn't make me happy, after all I was sixteen. They always tried to arrive after the newsreels because they were full of Nazi propaganda. Most of the other *Luziens* just walked out when they didn't like the news. One evening, they guessed wrong. A reel was showing the *Wehrmacht* maneuvering in Poland. Even though Saint-Jean-de-Luz's *Kommandant* was seated in a nearby loge, Michel commented loudly, "Look, Pauline, the sign shows 1250 kilometers from Paris. That's where they should stay!" His remark left her terrified. She wished he would be more reasonable.

The following day two imposing *Feldgendarmerie* (German Military Police) came to the hotel. They asked to speak to the hotel owner's son. Papa was summoned. In halting French one policeman said, "We have been told that your son is an escaped prisoner."

"It can't be," calmly answered Papa, "he visited us for a while on vacation from Paris. Last night, he took the night train back to Paris. We probably won't hear from him for a while due to the way the mail has recently been handled!"

The dig to the way mail was disrupted in the occupied zone probably went way over the Germans' heads. Satisfied with Papa's answer they left.

A shaking, and very angry Papa started to look for Michel. When he found him, Papa, always so well controlled, screamed,

"Imbecile! You stupid idiot! On account of your bravado, you nearly got yourself caught! How can you be so selfish, not thinking of your family and the consequences? As soon as it gets dark, I am going to drive you to the farm. Do you hear me? You are to STAY there and not come back until I tell you it's safe. Don't you dare show your face again in Saint-Jean-de-Luz."

No matter what Papa said to his children at any age, none dared disobey him. Never had we seen Papa in such a state, but he was protecting his son and probably all of us.

The farm, on 300 acres of land, was five kilometers inland. It had been bought by my parents in the early thirties. A villa was built next to it for the younger Branquet children's use during the summers. It was located in a very remote area at the foot of the Pyrénées. The farm and villa were only accessible by an ill defined dirt road. France's countryside has countless *petits bouts du monde*, (little ends of the world). There are swarms of off-the-beaten-track roads and paths, impossible for the average person to find. Michel spent the rest of the occupation well hidden as a farmer. Our Spanish tenement farmers had returned to Spain after the revolution. Since then the fields had remained fallow.

We thought that it was the railroad ticket taker, a fierce registered communist, who had betrayed Michel to the

Germans. He knew that Michel was a rabid anti-communist. Informers are the plague of wars and conflicts. Sadly France had its share.

The Branquet family was leading a day to day existence. With our Basque resilience most of us adapted, without succumbing to our new conditions. But Papa was getting more and more excitable. When he talked, his hands moved constantly, like birds taking flight. After the Germans' arrival, his language had taken a different turn, new words punctuated his sentences depending on what he was *rouspéter* (griping) about. "Ah! *Mais ça alors* (But, really)!"

"Ah! *Merde alors* (Oh! Shit)!"

Other times, Papa would walk around, hands behind his back, muttering under his breath, shaking his head, repeating,

"Those *sales Boches* (dirty Krauts). They bug us, those bastards!"

It is in the shelter of each other that the people live.
–Irish proverb

Never give in. Never. Never. Never. Never!
–Sir Winston Churchill

Chapter 3

There is no security on earth, there is only opportunity.

–General Douglas MacArthur

In August Pauline and I wanted to attend our convent high school annual week-long spiritual retreat in Pau, now located in the unoccupied zone. Because of the travel restrictions between the two zones, we needed to apply for a *Ausweis*. We decided to try our luck. On a hot sweltering day, we walked to the *Kommandantur* located in a requisitioned small hotel on a street nearby. As we had never talked to a German, we were apprehensive about asking for the *Ausweis*. We didn't know how the Germans comported themselves. When we arrived at the *Kommandantur's* door we looked at each other.

Taking a deep breath I bravely told Pauline, "*Allons-y* (let's go)!"

As we approached a desk near the entrance, the soldier on duty glanced at us with a bored expression. He had dark short-cropped hair and pale blue eyes. Pauline asked for two application forms.

Impassively, the perspiring soldier picked up some papers and pushed them on the desk toward us. After carefully answering the endless questions, we handed the applications to the soldier and left.

Three days later we returned to inquire about the progress of our request. This time a smiling soldier was at the desk. We gave our name and asked for our *Ausweis*. He looked at a pile of papers, shuffled them and to our great disappointment gave us a brief, "*nein!*" Applications denied. With help from Maman, the refusal was not going to deter us from accomplishing what we wanted.

Daily, our newspaper, *Le Sud-Ouest*, listed the names of people who had been caught by the Germans crossing the invisible border clandestinely. The sentence was two weeks in a French jail. Being caught and jailed became a badge of honor, at least they had tried! No food was served, families had to bring meals to the incarcerated. The *Feldgendarmerie* used trained dogs to detect people sneaking through.

Despite these facts, Maman contacted a man recommended to her, who lived in the border town of Orthez. He helped people cross the demarcation line to the unoccupied zone and agreed to assist us. With the passage of time, and to this day, it is a mystery how Maman's strictness relaxed enough to allow us, unsupervised, to take such a risky adventurous journey. During those years of uncertainty and turmoil, was Maman trying to instill into her middle daughters the well known Basque spirit of independence, which was going to serve me well during the difficult, long occupation years? During my lifetime, it helped me face adversity and problems without giving up.

It was her greatest legacy to me! Maman was maybe showing her suppressed independent nature through us.

We boarded the train in Saint-Jean-de-Luz, our bicycles loaded in the baggage wagon. In Bayonne, we changed trains to a secondary line. Maman had told us that on arrival in Orthez, *Monsieur* LeBlanc would be waiting at the train station with his daughter Louise who was my age. We were to recognize them by Louise's white hat. After our arrival his instructions were very precise, "Keep your backpacks on your bicycle racks. Cover them with your sweaters. Pedal leisurely as though you are going to a picnic. Most of all act naturally, talk to each other, laugh."

His daughter Louise, and the two of us were to bicycle toward a road which was the demarcation line. It was heavily patrolled by the *Feldgendarmerie* who didn't venture into small paths. At a certain point we were to leave the road and take a side path well described by *Monsieur* LeBlanc. The path was protected on both sides by thick, tall hedgerows which would give us ample cover. Louise's instructions were to stay on the main road as a look out while we took the path. All went as planned, we had no trouble. What excitement for a teenager!

As we had missed the train to Pau, upon our arrival at the convent, the nuns were absolutely in awe of all the distance we had traveled on our bicycles, forty kilometers. Even though we were young, had a purpose and were determined, the bicycle trip had been long and tiresome. Pauline and I were the only pupils living in the occupied zone who had made it and had the *guts* to cross the demarcation line without papers. We were treated like adventurous heroes. During free time of the retreat I held the other students spellbound with the tale of our adventure, mimicking the *Kommandantur's* Germans to make the story more interesting. A daring journey which we would not have ever thought about even in our wildest dreams if not assisted by our Maman.

A week later it was time to return home. The process had to be done in reverse. The plans were that Louise would meet us at the end of the path leading to the same main road. The prearranged understanding was no signal everything okay, waving a red scarf–*Feldgendarmerie*. We saw the scarf! A car had appeared in the distance, and Louise pedaled away, waving at it. We immediately crouched behind the excellent camouflage of the hedgerows. After five minutes, I peeked. No German car! At top speed we pedaled toward the road. No one was in sight. The road was deserted. We found out later that Louise had lured the Germans around the bend of the road so we would not be seen. Overcoming her distaste, she had stopped the soldiers, engaging them in conversation. Who could resist talking to a pretty young French girl which was not a frequent occurrence? Her trick gave us enough time to pedal to the main road without being seen. What a "*tour de force* (a feat)!" We were so proud of Louise who had fooled the Germans. With her help, another victory added to our list!

Waiting behind the hedgerows I had asked Pauline, "What do we do if the Germans come in our direction?"

Smiling, she had quickly answered, "Pedal fast!"

"And if they shoot?" I quizzed her.

Laughing, she answered, "Pedal even faster."

Under these circumstances, what a sense of humor! Without being caught, shot at and pedaling fast, WE HAD MADE IT! We could not wait to get home and tell everyone about our adventure, and how the Germans had been outmaneuvered!

Slowly the summer came to an end. It was time to think of the fall term. How could we go back to school now that the convent was in the unoccupied zone? Maman decided that Pauline only would return to our school in Pau. Education and diplomas were necessary for a future nun-teacher. As for me, Maman declared that it was not essential to finish my secondary studies.

After all she said, "You have often not been a very attentive student. Your report cards invariably stated, '*Peut faire mieux* (Could do better)!'"

Over the years, I had been compared to Pauline. I thought, why try, she is more intelligent than me, behaves better and is a good student. Under a devil-may-care attitude I had hidden an overly sensitive nature. I remember vividly a childhood incident when I answered Papa after a severe scolding, "I don't care!" When I really did care deeply!

There were reasons it didn't come as a terrible blow. At sixteen years old, I could think of many others things I would rather do than return to the convent. The beach was always inviting, I loved to swim. The ocean was my element even in winter. But, deep down I was resentful that Pauline was selected to continue her studies, and I was left behind. Also we had never been separated. Surprisingly, Pauline was able to obtain a rare *Ausweis* from the *Kommandantur* to return to school. The Germans were totally unpredictable.

In those days, education for women who were destined to be married was not considered necessary. More important was to learn to sew, embroider and how to keep house, cook and be introduced to the social graces. Maman sent me to a local convent to learn how to embroider towels and sheets which would be part of my trousseau for when I would be betrothed. Without my knowledge, Maman had my future planned—marriage. She already had her eye on some local bachelors, the doctor, dentist or surgeon, for a future husband.

After Pauline's departure, Maman decided to have me volunteer at the winged wimple Sisters of Charity kindergarten to help them with the children.

My sister Anne, then age eleven, was sent to a boarding school convent ten kilometers north of Saint-Jean-de-Luz. She was too young not to go to school. Jean, my younger brother, age ten, was enrolled in an adjoining boys' boarding school.

Starting in October 1940, mail from foreign countries could not be received except in an emergency. Such mail would be handled by the International Red Cross. Mail between the occupied and unoccupied zones was reduced to pre-printed interzonal cards. Pauline and I would no longer be able to write to each other, and neither would Maman and her sister, my Godmother, who lived near Pau. The cards were available for purchase at the PTT (Postes, Téléphone et Télégraph, Post Office) or at tobacco shops where in France stamps are always available for purchase. Certain words were printed. One could fill in the empty spaces, cross out the words which didn't pertain to the skimpy messages. Only family matters were allowed on the cards. Any deviation would cause the card to be discarded. The Germans were afraid that information would be sent to the British through the mail.

Simplified example of a card

Date _____ 194

_____ health (one added good or bad, etc.),

_____ sick, wounded, prisoner, died (name of person) _____ returning from _____ no news of _____ Family is well. _____

____ is working ____ needs money ____ returning to school.

Love, kisses. Regards.

Signature _____

These nonsensical messages contained a minimum of information. Besides these cards, NO other mail was allowed between the two zones, and none was received except whatever could be smuggled. Within the occupied zone, letters were censored. After being opened the envelopes were sealed with tape on which the swastika emblem was imprinted. The lack of mail added to our isolation!

Adding to the tense situation was the plundering by the Germans who continued to methodically seize coal, gasoline, livestock, and many other supplies to feed the Third Reich. The main worry of the occupied French became, "How are we going to feed ourselves?" For my family and many others, in our little corner of the world it was not as yet a major problem.

On October 23, 1940, Hitler and Franco had a meeting planned which was going to take place ten kilometers south from Saint-Jean-de-Luz in Hendaye on the French side of the border with Spain. Hitler needed Franco's permission to march the *Wehrmacht* through Spain to invade Gibraltar, thus giving him access to Africa. Hitler also wanted Spain to join Germany and Italy in the war against the Allies.

Hitler's armored wagon had to pass through Saint-Jean-de-Luz. Only two rail lines are available from Paris to Madrid on each side of the Pyrénées Mountains. One on the Mediterranean in the east and one in the west on the Atlantic side. The latter one is the most direct route from Berlin to the Spanish border. On October 23, 1940 all train service between Paris and Hendaye was cancelled. Hitler and his staff slept in the train which was stopped in a tunnel between Saint-Jean-de-Luz and Hendaye. He felt safer than in the open.

French Basques, under occupation only four months, were given draconian orders, STAY HOME! Germans troops patrolled the streets of Hendaye and Saint-Jean-de-Luz. All access roads leading to the railway stations and the rails were guarded by armored cars, machine guns ready to fire. All whose houses faced the railroad tracks were ordered to have windows and shutters closed. German soldiers were posted on rooftops near the railway station, their weapons pointed and ready to shoot. Troops also lined the railway stations' concrete platforms, a precise ten feet apart, their backs to the rails until after the train had passed. Anything they saw moving would be shot at on the spot.

Franco had the audacity to make Hitler wait one hour and it turned out to be for nothing. Crafty Franco knew his country's weaknesses. Spain had been convulsed and just emerged from thirty-two months of atrocious, horrible and devastating fratricidal civil war. He was facing seemingly insurmountable problems to rebuild Spain. More than five hundred thousand Spaniards had died. Franco refused to be drawn into the war with Hitler and Mussolini. He advised the *Führer* that if Gibraltar was to be taken from the English, he was going to do it himself! Hitler left, furious with Franco's NO. But he was really too busy elsewhere to try to punish Franco for his refusal.

In that little corner of the world, the Third Reich's strength first saw its limits. The Pyrénées Mountains would keep Spain out of Hitler's clutches. The frontier was closed tight by the Germans, or was it?

As a teenager, I had no concept of the importance of that historical moment. Franco's NO averted the use of Saint-Jean-de-Luz's roads for the convenience of the *Wehrmacht* to cross into Spain on their way to Gibraltar then on to Africa. The NO probably saved my family, myself and many others in Saint-Jean-de-Luz and the Basque region from inevitable bombing by the Allies. History was in the making. Spain, by remaining neutral for the duration of the war, became a haven for people of all races and religions escaping Hitler's steely grip. Thanks to Franco's refusal the Pyrénées Mountains became a natural brake against the onrush of the *Wehrmacht*.

Franco chose to close his eyes to the numerous Allied Air Force pilots, crew members, communists, political dissidents, escaped prisoners of war, Jews and people of all nations forced to escape between 1940-44 through the Pyrénées on their way to England. All of them escaping Nazi persecution.

In early October German U-boats continued to torpedo unarmed civilian boats. The Empress of Britain, a British ocean liner on its way to Canada, was sunk. Most of its passengers were rescued, among them many children.

For the first time in twenty-two years, we were not allowed to celebrate November 11, World War I Armistice day. To the French people's consternation and disgust, Vichy-France abolished our cherished national anthem, *La Marseillaise*.

"*Allons enfants de la Patrie, le jour de gloire est arrivé* (Let's go children of the homeland, the day of glory has arrived)."

Maybe it was just as well, the day of glory was gone. It was replaced by a song in honor of Field Marshal Pétain! "*Maréchal, nous voilà* (Marshal, here we are)!" We refused to sing the new despised national anthem.

On November 11, 1940 there were protests by Paris students. They distributed flyers in high schools, colleges and to faculties.

"Students of France, November 11 is still a national holiday. Despite orders from the occupation forces, you will not attend classes. You will honor the Unknown Soldier. All students stand together so France will live."

Students also showed their defiance by laying flowers on the tomb of the unknown soldier under *l'Arc de Triomphe* located at the end of the *Champs-Elysées* in Paris. It was the first open revolt against the Germans. The French Police helped the Germans to quell the rebellion. Some students died.

German soldiers had to be stationed near major posters to protect them from being torn down! Parisians have always been full of mischief.

Cousin Olga's frequent letters told stories about the capital. She wrote about her neighborhood's photography shop window displaying a large photograph of Pétain with a sign, *Vendu* (traitor). Germans were rarely seen in her area, and didn't care about Frenchmen's opinions about the unoccupied zone president.

She related a true amusing story. An elderly Frenchwoman would often walk with a cane on the *Champs-Elysées*. When a soldier was close by she would purposely trip him with her cane. She then would profusely apologize.

The news was, more often than not, very sad. But with her extraordinary sense of humor Olga often softened the bad news. She was not always successful! She once sent a newspaper clipping, "First civilians have been executed by the Germans for acts of violence against a member of the *Wehrmacht*."

...the horrible consciousness of waste...
—Eleanor Roosevelt, Pacific tour, 1943
from The Eleanor Roosevelt Story, *Archibald MacLeish*

Chapter 4

Er lebt wie Gott in Frankreich (He lives like a God
in France).

–German saying

Another season of my youth stolen. During the later part
of the year, we didn't know that the German High Command was formulating plans which were going to affect me
directly. They selected Saint-Jean-de-Luz as a R & R (Rest
& Recreation) location for their soldiers. The town's
Kommandant was ordered to find a hotel suitable for their
needs. Hôtel de la Poste, one of the largest in town, had
eighty-five rooms and was located on the main national
road. The Germans' choice of my parents' hotel was the
loss of the only home I had ever known, the home where
I was born. German requisition orders changed peoples'
lives from one day to another. The result of France's defeat
due to its politicians lack of insight.

Privately, I cried in anger at the stealing of my home.
The *Boches* would spoil it with their presence. In our little
corner of the world, one of Hitler's tentacles strangled my
parents' business and destroyed it. It was a complete

upheaval. I kept asking myself over and over again, like a broken record, "What kind of life are we going to lead now?"

The few remaining clients of the Hôtel de la Poste had to be relocated in smaller hotels which had not been requisitioned. While we were getting the hotel ready, the *Oberleutnant* returned with additional instructions. We would not be completely thrown out! We could live in a seldom used small apartment of no use to them. It was located on the ground floor of the hotel's newest wing, with a separate entrance through a lovely small, enclosed private garden which bordered *rue Gambetta*. The apartment, however, was too small to accommodate my sister Marie and her family. Luckily, even on such short notice an apartment was located down the street.

Further orders were received: All connecting hallways between the hotel and apartment had to be boarded twice with double strong partitions. One on the Germans' side and one on ours. The verbal orders reinforced the original requisition orders that the hotel had to remain as it was, with all its equipment, kitchen utensils, linens and employees. Our *maitre d'hôtel* (headwaiter), Raymond, who had worked in the hotel for twenty years resigned immediately. A few employees elected to leave as they didn't want to work for the *Boches*. Others remained for different reasons, mainly, they needed their jobs. They had families to feed. Twenty-four hours was not much time to move and comply with the various German demands.

Later that afternoon I heard pounding from the street. With my inquisitive nature I had to find its source. As I slowly walked out I sadly saw several soldiers hoisting the despised Nazi flag with its iron cross and swastika on a newly installed pole onto the outside of the hotel's wall near the entrance. It would remain at that spot for the duration of the occupation.

The ensuing twenty-four hours were spent moving and without sleep. In the linen room we looked for the oldest sheets to make the beds. Eighty-five bedrooms had to be prepared. On the fourth floor, Anne helped me use one sheet only per bed folding the bottom in half. We were sure that the German soldiers coming for R & R would be delighted to have a clean bed to sleep in, no matter how many sheets were on them. This way we were able to save more of the hotel linens. They might think that the French, an inferior race, made their beds differently! How we giggled!

Later a sharp looking officer with penetrating, huge dark eyes came to inspect our progress. As I was walking on the second floor landing, my arms full of towels, he stopped me. In passable French, he commented on the good view from the back entrance of the hotel.

Boldly I replied, "Yes, a good view of the cemetery!"

The Germans were puzzled by the Basque cross that adorned the hotel's beautifully carved wooden staircase. They thought it was a swastika. It is an old emblem found on some Basque houses in the country and on old headstones in cemeteries.

Basque cross

A three-star hotel, Hôtel de la Poste's restaurant dishes were porcelain of Limoges; serving plates, tea and coffee pots, place settings were sterling silver. We could not possibly leave all of them to the *sales Boches* (dirty Krauts). During the night Papa loaded the car and drove to the villa five kilometers away with a lot of linen. After his return, he took off again, the car crammed with copper pots to hide at Maman's brother's house in Orègue, a little speck of a cheerful village hidden in one of the most inland, remote parts of the Basque country, population of maybe 100 or less. As late as 1940, cars were rarely seen on their only unpaved main road.

One area with stone flooring in the hotel was called *les bicyclettes* where bicycles were stored and other paraphernalia. In its large closet, we squeezed as much silverware as we could. After the door was removed, a plasterer soccer friend of my brother Michel sealed it, and an old, broken refrigerator was placed in front of it. No one would know what was sealed in the wall except us! In a second floor hotel bedroom, the parquet floor was lifted and more silver hidden. The Germans would sleep in that room, and walk on a floor of silver. If they only knew!!

How exhausted we were! Still more had to be done. At the south side of the hotel was located a large cellar only accessible from the street down a couple of steps. Its existence was naturally not divulged to the Germans. Papa decided to use it to store the hotel food supplies; flour, canned goods, and oil. The dirt floor of the cellar was dug up and cases of sardines were buried.

During those twenty-four hours my vitality was devoted to transportation. I was nominated the runner for small items. A package would be handed to me and I had to run the whole length of the hotel to the cellar. On account of the curfew we had to be very careful. When Papa or someone else carried heavy packages I was the lookout. If a German was sighted in the vicinity, I was to warn the others by whistling the first bar of the Basque song, *Nere etchea, ikhusten duzu goizean* (Do you see the morning)? It was the one time Maman didn't object to my unladylike whistling.

Depending on where anyone was, we had three choices, continue running forward, return or, the worst, get caught for breach of curfew. Many close calls, but we didn't get apprehended. Never had so few people worked so hard to do so much in such a short time and in harmony.

When that immense undertaking was finished, Pauline and I had to think of our personal belongings. We rushed to our bedroom where it didn't take us long to throw our clothes together. We were used to living like nomads, moving, giving up our bedrooms every summer for clients, going to boarding school and the country villa. We didn't own anything superfluous.

I could not accept these strangers, the *Boches*, intruders and enemies, who in one day had taken my home. They would now sleep above in my bedroom and MY BED. It troubled me no end. What did they think? What were their dreams? Many soldiers, I am sure, would have preferred to be at home with their families and sleep in their own beds. Such feelings naturally were not attributed to the SS, the already dreaded Gestapo, and many of the officers faithful to the Nazi regime.

Our new life started, and was immediately very different in many aspects. Maman, and even at times Papa, began to cook. A sight I had never seen.

Every evening everyone's shoes had to be polished, one of my chores. Even when Pauline was around it also fell upon me to do the family ironing which was quite a lot. She had no inclination toward housework of any kind, and Anne was too young. I was really born at the wrong time; chores upon chores fell upon my silently protesting and rebellious shoulders. With such a large family chores seemed endless. It was not fair! I resented it!

I continued helping the nuns at the kindergarten, and attending my sewing classes.

One balmy night, Pauline and I were getting ready for bed. She closed the latticed shutters of our new bedroom. Windows could stay open, cool temperatures were not upon us as yet. Watching her, I started giggling. She had not noticed that a soldier's pair of pants hanging, probably to dry from the balcony above was caught by the closed shutters. What a funny sight! When Pauline turned around she saw me laughing so hard that I was crying. I could only point my finger toward the window. We happily left the pants caught and instantly fell asleep. Sweet dreams for us after playing another trick on the Germans.

Bright and early, we were awakened by loud, fast German spoken from above. By the tone of the soldier's voice we knew that he was more than angry about his pants. We could only detect the usual *Franzosen* (French) often repeated. Was it with obscenities? Probably better that we didn't understand the words. We saw the pants being pulled from our closed shutters until finally we heard a delightful ripping sound. How wonderfully funny! We burst out laughing and chalked up another victory.

A while later we heard the door bell ring. We didn't dare get up as we knew that we were in trouble and it would not take long until Papa would march into our bedroom. An unshaven, angry, bold German soldier was at the apartment door. With a gruff voice and through clenched teeth, he had rattled off rapid German holding up the ripped pants. Papa, shrugging his shoulders answered him, "*Nicht spagen sie Deutsch* (I don't understand German)!"

Then Papa slammed the door in his face. Soon we heard Papa's angry voice shouting, and the sound of his steps on the parquet floor, "Maita, Pauline where are you?" When he walked into our bedroom, we feigned blissful sleep. He roared, "Get up!"

Pauline obeyed immediately. Slowly opening my eyes, rubbing them and stretching, I added my two francs, "*Pourquoi*, Papa (Why, Papa)?" Over the years my multitudes of *pourquois* (whys) had driven Papa to distraction. In our family questions would, most of the time, be answered by, "I don't have to tell you why."

I took my time getting out of bed. Exasperated Papa roared, pulling the sheets off my bed, "Really, Maita are you deaf? Get up!"

Standing in front of him in our white nightgowns, trying to look innocent and sorry at the same time, we waited. Papa gave us a half-hearted scolding, just to save face. His daughters had guts! For us it was another feather in our caps! Continuing our private war!

In our little corner of the world, for the Germans on R & R billeted at the Hôtel de la Poste, it was a vacation at the seashore. So far away from where the front had been. Despite their uniforms they looked like sightseers, cameras hanging from their necks, gawking at the sights. Most of them probably had never been out of Germany.

Hôtel de la Poste dining room before the Germans' requisition and during their stay with a swastika painted on the wall (below).

One employee told Papa that German nurses were now permanently stationed at the hotel to care for the soldiers' minor medical problems. He also said that one of the dining room walls had a large swastika painted on it. Some of the tables had been pushed aside to make room for ping pong tables.

As the soldiers were on R & R they didn't have much to do. Most afternoons they would take long naps. When my younger siblings were home from school we waited for that time to start playing in our garden, making as much noise as possible, shouting and shrieking. I had been blessed with a powerful set of lungs, and had found an excuse to put them to good use. In different circumstances we would have been reprimanded as we had been taught to respect people's privacy. During these extraordinary times, my parents mostly chose to overlook our bad manners toward the Germans! To all of us, they were not people, but intruders who were living in our hotel taken by force and taking away our livelihood. Shutters and windows would open, fists would be shaken and angry German words would come tumbling down on us. As usual, we could only understand the word, *Franzosen.* What a ball making the German soldiers uncomfortable!

At times, they would try to appease us by throwing down candy and oranges which we had not seen in stores for quite a while. To no avail...we would throw them back at them, spit or stomp on them. Maman had warned us that such foods were probably poisoned! Windows and shutters would close again with a loud clatter. It didn't bother us a bit. On the contrary, we loved it! What could those soldiers do? Nothing! They were ordinary soldiers on R & R, a mixture of all branches of the German Armed Forces with no authority. Their superiors had more important things to do than bother with some incorrigible French children who were not sub-humans, but still not of the Aryan race. They had been instructed to be *correct* with the French. They needed us. Oh! What fun we had!

The tribute extracted from France by the Third Reich was exorbitant, resulting in more and more shortages. Supplies and staples rapidly disappeared. Each week tons were diverted toward Nazi Germany. Still huge quantities of goods never reached the consumers, the best of the leftovers was diverted to the black market.

To add to the nation's problems many unscrupulous French people profited at the expense of others. The black market was in full swing selling meat, eggs, milk at five times the official prices. France sprouted a new class of society called, *nouveaux-riches* (new rich). The hardest hit were people on fixed incomes, white collar workers, the retired and the elderly who could not afford the outrageous prices. None had bartering power. Also affected were the prisoners' of war wives who no longer had a wage earner in the family. The saddest part was that the real black marketeers peddled their wares without punishment and the poor people would appear in front of judges for stealing a loaf of bread, an egg or some cheese. It was worse than in the Middle Ages. Stolen or counterfeit ration cards could be bought, but only at a premium. The penalty by the Germans for counterfeiting was DEATH.

Before the war France had always been a self-sufficient country producing enough staples for its population which was around forty-two million. Now its larger cities' inhabitants were starving, they had insurmountable problems. Even though the Salvation Army was suspended in France, in Paris soup kitchens continued helping many people. Solidarity had not stopped. Help came from the Red Cross, nameless benevolent organizations and from the courage of individuals ready to help their neighbors.

Everyone was thinking about FOOD. Would I eat white crusty bread, pastries or chocolate ever again? I could only dream.

Shortly after we were evicted, a lean, more than six foot tall *Feldgendarmerie* policeman with bright blue eyes and a strong chin came to our apartment asking for the hotel owner. As usual I had been the first one to answer the doorbell, someone interesting might be there. Very politely I asked him to wait then ran to find Papa, who came back to the door with me grumbling, "Ah! *Merde alors* (Oh. Shit)! What does he want?"

He wanted the key to the cellar. How could the Germans have found out? Probably an anonymous informer or a disgruntled hotel employee! It was quite a blow! All those so badly needed supplies were now going to feed those *Boches*. Papa had no choice! The only good part was that they didn't find the cans of sardines buried under the dirt floor!

Due to my vivacious, full of curiosity personality I still found *fun* in daily living. There were always interesting things to see and do. Maman would often say that I always had one foot off the ground, ready to go.

"He who laughs last, laughs longest."

–Homer's *Iliad*

Since I was no longer going to school, my first cousin Léon, a year older, and I were often together and he became my closest playmate and friend. If you saw one, the other would be close by. We were buddies. His father's garage and small pension were down the street from the hotel. One of our favorite pastimes was to stand in front of the garage looking at the Boches passing by. We could always find something about them to laugh about or make some derogatory remarks.

On a boring overcast day, a young German soldier with short dark cropped hair, looking not much older than Léon, approached us. He asked a question. On account of his heavy accent we didn't really understand him. Puzzled, we looked at each other trying to guess. Turning toward Léon, shrugging my shoulders I asked him, "Do you think he said, Ohlette, that he wants to go there?" Ohlette is but a small area, part of the village of Urrugne at the foot of the Pyrénées where our country villa is located.

"Why would he want to go there?" questioned Léon with a puzzled expression.

"I don't know," I retorted, but opted for my guess. To the soldier I answered, "Three kilometers," using three fingers for clarity.

He looked aghast, then gestured for Léon to follow him. In a corner of the garage, he showed Léon what he wanted. He had asked us directions to the toilettes!! To us in his French with a heavy German accent, it sounded the same as Ohlette! No wonder that my answer of three kilometers had shocked him. His first thought must have been. Those crazy Franchozen to install toilets three kilometers away! Nevertheless, he had been considerate and respectful of me. Léon directed him to the public toilets. Smiling, the young soldier left saying, "*Danke schon* (Thanks a lot)."

Our new kitchen windows overlooked a small lovely public park located behind the hotel. It was well shaded by beautiful *platanes* (plane trees). At times, when Léon came to the apartment, we watched a sight that always amused us. The German soldiers practicing the goose-step. Officers would bark guttural orders, the soldiers in unison would react like marionettes with invisible persons pulling their strings. Stiff legs would go up and down. They looked so ridiculous!

Our favorite sight was when the Germans were marched to the beach. The soldiers wore only white shorts, probably their undershorts, but with a must everywhere they went, their highly polished black boots. The cameras were not forgotten, and would swing to rhythm of their steps. They would leave the hotel, in formation, singing the same strange song. Even with the passage of forty-nine years I can still vividly remember the tune. The words sounded to us like, *Ali, Alo, salaud* (Go to the water, bastards). Bastard, a word at that time I was not familiar with, especially with my strict convent upbringing. Léon didn't take long to enlighten me. How we loved that, to us, an absurd song! It is not until recently that in passing I asked a German acquaintance if she knew the song. After I hummed it, a smile crossed her face, "I know it. It's an old German army marching song repeating, 'Heidi ido ida with emphasis on the last a of ida, heidi ido ida, heidi ido ida' repeated three times. The equivalent of singing la, la la then emphasis on two more la la and again and again." We had a good laugh.

A great part of the beach was reserved for the Germans, absolutely—*VERBOTEN*—signs had been posted. When we went swimming in our area we would watch them. All boots had to be lined up neatly, and following a sharp order, the soldiers had to jump in unison into the sea. The Germans were obsessed with *ordnung* (order). They believed that without order in the most minute things, chaos takes over! They had a passion for order and precision, the famous Germanic habit of thoroughness.

With kind permission of *Madame* Aubert, France.
Ordnung *(order)*. Germans' *military boots aligned on the beach.*

Often the swimming was followed by a speech from an officer. He probably was telling them again and again how great their *Führer* was and how soon the war would be won by the Third Reich! Another of their pastimes on the beach was horseback riding on stolen French horses.

One spring day, my little brother, Jean, then twelve and Papa were walking on the beach collecting sea shells. Jean, an overly active child was running with clenched fists after the strutting seagulls making them take flight. A German soldier, his thick blond hair rumpled from swimming, ran toward Jean and apprehended him thinking that he was doing the communist salute! Papa was able to convince him that his son was just playing. "Really," Papa said later recounting the incident, "it was ridiculous. Didn't he have anything better to do than to worry about a young boy's behavior?"

The occupation forces continued to have a hard time dealing with the unruly French people and especially their children. After that incident, Jean was terrified of the Germans. It became effective whenever he didn't behave, which was often, to be threatened with a phone call to the *Kommandant*. Papa found out later that a Frenchman had been shot in Bordeaux for doing the clenched fist communist salute during a *Wehrmacht* parade.

Léon and I loved to take off on our bicycles. One of our favorite promenades was pedaling to Ascain, six kilometers inland to visit *Parrain* (my godfather), *Curé* (pastor) Ibarrart of the Catholic Church. It was a small country village of about ten houses and a hotel. The rest consisted of colorful red tiled roofs over whitewashed Basque farmhouses scattered in the hilly green Pyrénées. *Parrain* was called *Tonton l'Abbé* (Uncle the Abbot) by his multitude of nieces and nephews. Every Sunday after Mass many farmers left supplies at the rectory so his larder was always well stocked! At our age we were always hungry, especially since the occupation. We knew that some goodies would always be available at the rectory.

He was a bald, short, jolly man with the most deep, infectious laugh and a quick wit. When he walked he always seemed to be in a hurry, his overcoat cassock flying behind. He cared deeply for his parishioners. Parrain would visit them by bicycle or on foot since his car tank was now empty of gas. It took some special preparations. Before he would get on his bicycle he had to gather his cassock, and hold the folds with clothespins so they wouldn't get tangled in the bicycle spokes. He was quite a sight! Even though Parrain was known for his lengthy sermons delivered in Basque, he was beloved by his parishioners. His house-keeper, Panchika, was an old maid fond of the bottle, but what a cook! Parrain would mark her bottles, keeping track of how much she drank. It didn't slow her drinking.

Parrain had a large vegetable garden well tended by Panchika, and fruit trees. Apple season, because I was the most agile, he would ask me to gather them. When he was not in sight I would shake the tree, making my job easier. I can still see him looking up, his glasses sliding down his nose, "Maita, you shook the tree."

Smiling down innocently, my answer would follow easily, "Oh! *Non, Parrain!*"

He would walk away shaking his head, mumbling, knowing full well that I was lying. Being his godchild gave me license to get away with these little lies and scenarios. We both loved it. I had always told him that never would I let him hear my confession. At that age, how many serious sins could one have? But I didn't want him to hear my personal failings and know that sometimes I told little white lies to him outside the confessional. He would also let me wrap up the coins collected at the Sunday Masses.

Reminiscing! He was what I consider a true priest. He lived simply and most of his cassocks and other clothes were purchased by Maman. Before the occupation, he would regularly come to eat lunch at the hotel with the family. To the great annoyance of Maman, Papa would often tease him unmercifully, "Go ahead, Father drink a little more wine."

After lunch he would read his breviary, walking back and forth in our dining/living room. As a child I would pick up the coat which was over his cassock and hold it like a train, marching behind him trying to mimic the whispering of his prayers which he read in Latin. It was hard at that age to consider him a man, because his cassock looked like a long dress. He was a wonderful, and kind godfather.

One sunny fall day, returning home from Ascain, Léon and I were happily pedaling next to each other on the careless road, chatting, laughing, not holding the handlebars, my hair flowing in the gentle breeze. We were savoring our freedom. Two teenagers with not a care in the world. A car passed us, stopped and backed up. It was the *Feldgendarmerie!* A huge German military policeman with hawk like eyes stepped out of the *verdigris* car shouting, "*Halt* (stop)!"

With universal sign language we were told first, it was *verboten* to bicycle side by side, and second, *verboten* to ride without holding the handlebars. We were instructed to continue our journey behind each other. After their reprimand we were each handed a PV, *Procès Verbal* (traffic ticket) to be paid at the Saint-Jean-de-Luz's *Kommandantur.*

Impatiently we got back on our bicycles, silently cursing those interfering idiots! Rules, rules! Oh! all those petty rules. Were they afraid that bicycling next to each other we might discuss the overthrow of the Nazi empire? No, they were sticklers for rules and obsessed with *ordnung* for the French and themselves! RULES must be obeyed by all! No sooner were they out of sight than we happily broke the rules again! When we got home we gave our respective fathers the tickets. Because we had no allowances—they paid! I can still see Papa digging in his pocket for the money muttering, "What next with my impetuous daughter?"

Laughter is the brush that sweeps away the cobwebs of the heart.

—Mort Walker, *King Features*

Chapter 5

What do we live for, if it is not to make life less difficult for each other.

–George Eliot

Ascain, on the border with Spain, was heavily occupied by the Germans. The only hotel and some private residences had been requisitioned. Odile, who later became my friend, lived in that village and recollects:

"We lived a slow-motion life, no transportation except bicycles. To better our menus, we would go to the surrounding farms to buy vegetables. The black market had made it hard, but we knew which farms to go to.

"Young people would escape to Spain through Ascain to join the French army exiled in Africa. Sadly, I remember one day seeing on the village square some young men flanked by the *Feldgendarmerie*. We assumed that they had failed in their attempt to cross the border. I have always wondered what happened to them and if they were sent to a concentration camp.

"My brother-in-law Pierre, a close friend of your brother Michel, was arrested and released within a month. We never knew until after the liberation that he had been a link in the underground helping people to cross the border to Spain. He was in the same network as your brother and your godfather's assistant, Father Iturbi, and our town hall secretary.

"Once, a Jewish man desperately needed to escape to Spain. He was directed to the rectory. Father Iturbi took him across the street to the church were he was dressed as an altar boy. He accompanied your godfather on foot to a far away farm, ringing a bell as was the custom when bringing the last rites to a dying person. There he was handed over to a Basque guide who helped him cross the Pyrénées to Spain. The escape was successful.

"A couple, *Monsieur* and *Madame* Larréguy, owners of a restaurant at the mountain pass named *Col de Saint-Ignace* were betrayed and arrested. They were a link in the same network as my brother-in-law Pierre. *Madame* Larréguy died in a concentration camp, her husband survived."

In our little corner of the world, the fact that in Saint-Jean-de-Luz most of the Germans were on R & R made the occupation a lot easier than it was for the rest of France. Most of them were regular troops who seemed polite and decent men. They had an air of passivity and were not often seen laughing. New arrivals were told not to touch the local women unless they were willing. The officers controlled the troops very firmly, and infractions were severely punished. A local woman was raped. It came to the attention of the *Kommandant* and the soldier was immediately shipped back to Germany.

The owner of Saint-Jean-de-Luz's best pastry shop, *Madame* Jauréguy, whose husband was a prisoner of war, hated the Germans. One day a lone German soldier walked into her shop. He wanted to buy a bottle of liquor. She refused, explaining that bottles could only be bought at a liquor store but offered to sell him a small glass. He insisted, she again refused. After the third "NON," he got mad! On a shelf behind her were neatly aligned bottles of various liqueurs and cognacs. He made her open all of them and fill small glasses from each bottle. Without saying a word he drank one glass, and of course, left without paying. He could have broken them all, but that would not have been correct, or following *ordnung*. Such a breech of discipline by the occupation forces in our little corner of the world was not tolerated.

It seemed that our door bell was ringing much too often. One day as it was ringing with insistence I ran to the front door, swung the door open. A German officer with an air of confidence and arrogance was facing me. He was tall with sleek black hair, and a white scar on his left cheek. Probably a remainder of a cadet sword duel which were common in the prewar German military academies. Speaking excellent French with a heavy clipped accent he politely said, "*Je voudrais voir Monsieur Branquet* (I would like to see Mr. Branquet)."

I asked him to wait a moment while I ran to find Papa. Run, run a habit that has never left me. We both returned shortly, a frustrated Papa walking in front of me toward the front door. With my inquisitive nature and voracious curiosity, I stayed nearby. I didn't want to miss a word of their conversation.

"*Monsieur* Branquet, I am Colonel Protzit. I have been told that you have a well stocked wine cellar. I would like to see it and choose some bottles."

Papa was stunned. How could he have known? Maybe the same informer who had divulged the location of the cellar had given him the information. Poor Papa had no choice but to get the key and show the treasured bottles which had taken him years to acquire. It broke Papa's heart to have this *cochon* (pig), like he was going to call him from then on in front of anyone who wanted to hear, drink his good wine.

Over the years, Papa had developed a natural connoisseur's taste. From one sip of wine and the smell, closing his eyes he could tell what vineyard the wine came from. With the passage of time I can still vividly see Papa drink his after lunch cognac, warming the glass with his cupped hands and slowly takings sips. When I was old enough, and only once in a while, I was allowed to dip a sugar cube in his glass and let the combination of cognac and sugar melt in my mouth. The delicious flavor and warmth would flow down my throat. What a treat and delicacy!

Colonel Protzit became a regular, unwelcome sight at our front door always leaving with his free requisitioned bottles. Papa never invited him in and assumed that Protzit never divulged the source of his wine supply, probably he didn't want to share. Colonel Protzit became a another word to scare Jean and my nieces, "If you don't behave, we are going to call Protzit."

After one of his exasperating visits, his bottle under his arm, Colonel Protzit who towered over my Papa said crisply, "*Monsieur* Branquet, Basque girls are not very polite toward our soldiers, especially your two daughters."

Smiling Papa replied, "I am very proud of it! And I wish you were not here!"

"So do I, *Monsieur* Branquet, so do I. I would rather be with my family in Bavaria."

It's a known fact that Basques have reserved natures. One didn't see Basque young women willingly talk to the German soldiers.

Besides answering our door for Colonel Protzit's unwelcome frequent visits I had no contact or conversations with Germans. Papa had some and it was not from his own choice.

Most weekends the troops in the hotel were entertained with concerts. Beautiful classical music would float through the partitions. It was my introduction to classical music.

A joke floated around town stating that the mandatory curfew imposed by the Germans was to make sure that everyone was home on time to listen eagerly to the forbidden BBC. The nightly French broadcasts started with the opening bars of Beethoven's Fifth Symphony which echoes the Morse code V for Victory: ••• - ••• -. The station call was, "*Ici, Londres* (Here, London)."

It became a signal to resist the Nazis. Despite the interference, crackling static and jamming by the Germans, we could understand most of the words. When the broadcasts were too garbled we needed to have our ears glued to the speaker. As we never knew when Colonel Protzit or a German would arrive at our door, we had to be careful and keep the volume very low. One of us always stood ready to change stations in case someone rang the doorbell. Anyone caught listening to the VERBOTEN BBC broadcasts was subject to arrest and imprisonment.

Daily, strange messages were heard. We learned later that they were addressed to the French underground, La Résistance.

"My aunt is not well, she will call you on Thursday. Is your larder empty? Have you seen Charlie? My aunt has finished her knitting. Uncle Felix went to see his mother. Molière does not smoke." Seemed that poor aunt was often mentioned. These messages were of great importance, and the answers radioed back to England greatly helped the Allies.

A current and very popular melancholic song was often heard on regular French radio programs, "I will wait day and night, I will always await your return." It referred to the prisoners of war returning! It was often whistled by Frenchmen in the streets.

In September 1940, my young sister Anne had to be rushed to the hospital with an appendicitis attack. Because night nurses were not available, a family member needed to spend the nights with her. As usual, I was the only one available to help. But, what about the curfew? Anne knew that I waited until the last minute to leave home. Every evening she would worry that I would not arrive on time. I would pedal furiously across the bridge to our sister city, Ciboure, where the small private hospital was located. She recalls that, to entertain her, I would spend the evenings clowning around. Anne had to beg me to stop as it would hurt her stitches to laugh. Most nights the air raid sirens could be heard. It was kind of scary, but, they always turned out to be false alarms.

Anne told me stories about her life at the boarding school.

"At dinner time we had often just an egg and some chestnuts. When we had a bad chestnut, we had to raise our hand to get a replacement from the nun. I don't know why I traded jars of preserves sent by Maman for bread because the bread was not that tasty. At night, we slept with our coats on our beds like blankets. Sister Agnès told us it was in case of air raids. Really, it was because of the fuel shortage. The dormitory was not heated."

In October another poster appeared, one of many more to come signed by the *Oberfeldkommandant*.

"Widespread rumors are being circulated about the difficulties purchasing food supplies. Anyone spreading these absurd rumors which can disturb public security will be punished by forced labor up to fifteen years."

It was rather a weird order when store shelves were being emptied of their contents by the occupation forces and supplies shipped to Germany.

In November, *Le Sud-Ouest*, printed directives from our Mayor: "Ration cards will be issued at *Hôtel de Villes* (town halls). Dates will be announced later."

The first staple to be rationed was sugar: 750 grams per month. A catastrophe! French people used a lot of sugar in their breakfast of coffee and milk. Papa used so much sugar that we used to tease him that his spoon would stand up in his *café au lait* (coffee with mostly milk).

Directives followed one after another. Butcher stores had to close Wednesdays, Thursdays and Fridays and *Charcuteries* (pork butcher shops), Tuesdays and Fridays. Bread was sold one day old, it weighed more. Gone were our delicious croissants, and other crusty bread fresh out of the bakery ovens.

By December pure coffee was no longer available. It was an added catastrophe for the French as *café au lait*, and bread were their basic breakfast staples. Imaginations were put to good use. Ersatz coffee, now called *Café National* (national coffee) was being concocted with chicory, ground chestnuts, acorns or grilled barley, just about anything that would make black water with a remote resemblance to coffee! Not a day passed that Papa didn't gripe about the despicable, loathsome ersatz coffee. He would call it, *jus de chaussettes* (juice of socks). One had to be really addicted to caffeine to drink these black witches' brews. Herbal tea became popular. Some was made with dandelions which were growing in the wild. Those were plentiful, the Germans could not confiscate them.

The unoccupied zone governed by the Vichy regime fared better than we did in many ways. During the winter the American Red Cross distributed milk in Marseilles.

What really matters is what you do with what you have.
                                        –Shirley Lord

It is a queer life one leads in a modern war...everyday the same...mostly food, food in spite of all that is happening...every day food.
                                        –Gertrude Stein

Chapter 6

What does not destroy us makes us stronger.

–Nietsche

Another season of my youth stolen. Winter 1940-41 was exceptionally and brutally cold. Weather seems to always be worse in times of trouble, it added to the Germans' oppression. Temperatures that low had not been recorded for many decades. It was all the more unbearable due to the lack of fuel.

In January, a rare sight in Saint-Jean-de-Luz, snow fell soon followed by ice. One day Léon and I were carefully walking down *rue Gambetta* watching with glee some of the soldiers falling. They didn't like it! Then came my turn to fall on my *derrière* (backside). It was their turn to laugh at me! My dignity was offended because Léon also laughed. It didn't take long for him to land on his. It was quite a sight! Like we say in French, "One pokes fun always with pleasure toward the one we love!" Léon and I were even.

Bleak winter! In January, bread rations were reduced to 300 grams (about ten ounces) per day! It was such a difficult shortage for the French who are so fond of their main staple! Our ration cards had eight classifications depending on age and/or needs. The daily ration of meat, twenty-eight grams, was meager compared to the prewar consumption of 111 grams! Milk was no longer available for adults.

Rations per month in grams

Cheese, 200 grams—Butter or oil 400 grams—Ersatz coffee 300 grams—Pasta 250—Rice none—Soap, which foamed less and less—100 grams.

Queues in front of grocery stores were getting longer and longer. Housewives spent the better part of their days going from store to store, trying to buy staples to feed their families. Maman was no exception. I would often go with her, and it was so weird entering Felix Potin grocery store to be faced by mostly empty shelves. Before we left the house we had to make sure that we had newspapers for wrapping and empty bottles in case a shipment of oil had arrived. Large cities were the worst hit by the shortages.

Now, nothing was thrown away. Return of burned out light bulbs was necessary to buy another. An empty toothpaste tube had to be presented in order to purchase a new one.

At sixteen years old I had a voracious appetite. My daily bread ration was barely enough for my breakfast of *café au lait*, now without butter! But Maman would dole out my portions in three parts, leaving enough for the other meals. She would often hide extra little portions, probably part of her own, in the cupboard as we had no access to the immense hotel refrigerator now used by the Germans. The bread rations were the beginning of more to come. To increase the weight of bread some dishonest bakers added all sorts of things to the dough, even pieces of cord were found in some loaves! By then the bread was no longer white but grey. Often the bread was like putty! Sometimes during our meals, out of Papa's range of vision, I would make bread balls. The balancing act would then start! I placed my knife on a spoon curve. The bread ball was delicately placed on the knife's blade which was touching the table. With my fist I would hit the handle with full force hoping that the ball would stick to the ceiling. It did at times, but not for long. Those that missed would end on the table or floor. My antics were followed by severe scolding from Papa. I vividly remember his comments which would usually be the same, "Really Maita, stop it. You are driving me crazy!" He would admonish raising his voice, "And don't ever do that again!"

"*Oui*, Papa." I would always answer him with an innocent smile, planning the next prank. I am sure that I added many grey hairs to his head. But I know that he forgave me. Diversions were needed in our dull lives.

It was the first time in the Branquet family that a teenager was becoming a nonconformist, willing to shock her elders openly. I was the only one in our family ever to fall into the troublesome teen category. We lived in extremely changed circumstances. Rules that had applied to my older siblings were no longer valid or applicable. It was due to the breakdown of our usual family structure caused by the war, our defeat and the German occupation. We were living in a part of France where the government had ceased to exist. All of us at the mercy and whims of the German High Command located in Paris. Gone for me were the routines of school and my parents operating a successful hotel business. Nothing had prepared us for a life way beyond the norm, one that none of us could have imagined even in our worst nightmares.

On account of my brothers' and sisters' ages we were affected differently by the occupation. *Les petits* were five and six years younger than I. They continued their formal education. Mine was interrupted, never to be completed. I was no longer in daily contact with girls my own age in a school setting which is important to one's emotional growth. Of all the children in the family my life was most disrupted and, I believe, was the most marked psychologically.

Some parts of our daily life didn't change. As we were brought up in a strict Catholic atmosphere, regular attendance to Mass was a must. Even the smallest deviation of religious duties was an opportunity for Maman to lecture on the different aspects of our faith. Discipline and sacrifice were expected from all of us, and modesty for the girls was ingrained from childhood. Good manners had always been expected; the Germans were an exception. They didn't count.

As we were now living as a family, devotion routines together were new. Every evening, we knelt in the living room repeating very long prayers followed by the Rosary. Léon, most of the time with us, stayed in the back of the room with me, each of us sitting on our legs. Maman would often turn around to remind us that kneeling properly was a necessary sacrifice. As soon as she resumed the prayers, Léon and I would hit each other playfully trying to make one another burst out laughing. It never failed. As soon as Maman heard the commotion, without a look backward she would invariably admonish, "Maita, come in front!"

I would take my time, my slippered feet sliding on the parquet floor, sometimes purposely falling. Why not? Our lives were so constricted, so dull! Poor Maman no longer scolded so sternly.

One evening the family was gathered around the kitchen table finishing our sparse meal. My older sister, Marie, and her daughters were with us. It was easier for them to share our meal than for Marie to cook for herself and her small family. Her oldest daughter, Giselle, was running around the table driving everyone crazy as only a three year old can. "*Arrétes-toi* (stop it)!" *Attata* (Grandpa in Basque) sternly told her. His patience like most adults', since the occupation, was wearing thin.

No sooner had he finished his scolding than we heard loud knocking on the shutters. We all immediately stopped talking. Perplexed, we looked at each other. Who could it be at this hour, we asked ourselves? No one spoke. The pounding started again. Finally in exasperation, Papa shouted, "*Sacrebleu!* What's going on? Probably some *sales Boches* (dirty Krauts) with a complaint. What would they want at this hour?" He abruptly turned around, sharply ordering, "Maita, shut off the electricity."

Blackout had to be observed, infractions were severely punished by heavy fines. Papa cautiously opened the window toward the inside and slowly pushed the shutters out. He peered into the darkness until he heard a male voice, "*C'est moi, Paul* (It's me, Paul). I beg of you, open the door."

Startled, Papa turned around roaring, "*C'est Paul* (It's Paul)!"

We could not believe that Marie's husband, prisoner of war, was at our back door. Marie screamed and fainted scaring Giselle who started to cry.

Flashlight in hand, Papa rushed to the back door. He ushered Paul in. Paul was dressed in tattered clothes, so thin and pale. Everyone started to speak all at once. When we had finally revived Marie, she threw herself sobbing into Paul's arms, touching his face, trying to convince herself that it was not a dream. He tried to pick up Giselle, but she screamed! She didn't know her daddy, she had been so small when he had been drafted.

Giselle had always thought that our Papa was hers also. Jean, my younger brother, her uncle, only nine years older, had all along kept telling her, "He is my Papa, not yours!"

She would then ask him, "Where is my Papa?"

"He is a prisoner of war." Jean would impatiently reply.

His answer, we thought, didn't mean much to her. Still it must have made some sort of an impression. One day passing in front of the hotel with its immense despised Nazi flag Giselle had told her mother in a very serious voice, "We can't enter my house."

Like the last four Branquet children she had been born in the hotel. Wise for only four years old, she had added, "I better whisper, the *Boches* might put me in prison like Papa."

After all the hugging, and we had all calmed down, Paul narrated the practically miraculous story of his release. We listened entranced. Most of his friends lived in Biarritz where he was born. One of them, Robert was a lifeguard at the beach where waves can be very treacherous unless one is an excellent and strong swimmer. Because Robert had saved many Germans soldiers from drowning he was offered a monetary reward by the *Kommandant* of Biarritz.

Instead of money Robert requested the release of two of his friends, both prisoners of war in Germany. It was granted. The Germans could not do without such a valuable lifeguard! Luckily one of the prisoners was Paul. He arrived home in poor health from lack of adequate food and unsanitary conditions. Toward the end of his captivity, he had been sent to work on a farm to replace the farmer's son who had died at the front in 1940. There, finally, he had been able to have a better diet. Now both our men were home, Michel safely at the farm and now Paul. How happy we all were.

Paul had a hard time adjusting to civilian life and freedom. He had also worked at the hotel before the war. Unemployment in France was at a all time high. Due to lack of supplies many businesses had to close their doors. Paul could not work in another hotel as most of them had been requisitioned by the Germans, nor could he find other work.

More edicts in the occupied zone! Some would be handed down through remnants of French authorities like town mayors.

Avis officiel (Official announcement)
Order from the German authorities

"Anyone hiding escaped prisoners of war or helping the enemy; downed Allied airmen, paratroopers, will be punished severely."

Even though the frontier with Spain was closed during the occupation, the Basque Country's classic *contrebandiers* from both sides of the rugged Pyrénées Mountains continued their centuries old trade. Throughout France Basques had always been known as smuggling specialists and often went to Spain without using conventional roads. During the occupation they used the mastery of ruse, and furtive crossing, skills that had been passed on from father to son. They knew the mountains intimately, and how and where to hide from the customs agents, and now from the Germans. Before the war they smuggled livestock, fabric, and chocolate. It was routine work. Now they smuggled desperate human beings fleeing persecution, certain suffering and probable death.

By early 1941 well organized escape routes were already in operation. Over one of these, during the next three-year period, more than one thousand people were successfully smuggled to freedom over the Pyrénées Mountains. These *contrebandiers* became lifesavers for people of many nations, and religious beliefs, who were escaping Hitler's steely tentacles. They helped downed Allied airmen, Jewish people and many others. Besides the *contrebandiers*, guides and sheepherders were familiar with the mountains as well as lumbermen, and many hunters like my father and brother Michel. Some French women volunteered to escort the escapees to safe houses, pretending to be their wives so they would be less conspicuous. Others would bicycle to farms, pretending they were merely on their way home.

By mid-year, a *Réseau* (network) was in operation using Saint-Jean-de-Luz as the base. The *canton* (subdivision containing a group of towns) of Saint-Jean-de-Luz was a section on the Basque coast with easy access, especially being on the rail line Paris-Madrid. One recorded famous escape was of a Jewish couple. On a horse drawn flat cart the husband was laid on a mattress, and covered with blankets. His head and part of his face were bandaged. His wife, dressed in a white nurse's uniform with the red cross on her veil, sat next to him. He supposedly was being taken back, after his stay in the hospital, to their farm at the foot of the Pyrénées. When they arrived at the designated Basque farm, they were smuggled to Spain. Escapes were an exhausting process for everyone, especially for people who were not used to walking in difficult, dangerous and steep terrain. As one goes away from the coast, the Pyrénées Mountains get higher and higher. Not all attempted escapes were that successful. Many people died trying, together with their helpers.

In the twenties and early thirties, crossing the border was taken for granted, an everyday experience. Passports were not required. Because clothes were much cheaper in Spain, we often went with Papa and Maman on shopping trips. We would wear old clothes and return wearing new ones down to our shoes so we carried no packages to declare. No one ever thought that it was wrong, it was the custom. I remember clearly the Spanish in Irun and the French customs agents in Hendaye on both sides of the bridge dutifully asking my parents and others crossing by car or on foot if they had anything to declare. The answer was always, no. They all knew that it was not true! Another time I crossed the bridge with yards of fabric wrapped around me under my clothes.

March 1941 brought sadness. A British Air Force Lancaster was shot down on one of the pocket size beaches along the Basque coast. The beach, Erromardi, three kilometers from Saint-Jean-de-Luz was ordered off limits for the duration of the occupation. We would miss it, we'd had many picnics on that lovely small, sandy beach tucked between high cliffs. Two bodies were retrieved. A funeral service was conducted in our church. A German officer attended, and after the Mass he spoke to our pastor, "We are enemies now, but after death we are all the same." Sundays, German soldiers and officers would be seen attending various Masses.

Basque churches are unique because men and women do not sit together. In Saint-Jean-de-Luz Church, men sat in three tiered galleries. On the ground floor, women sat on caned chairs or knelt at low kneelers, also caned. School children sat on benches. Women were not supposed to enter churches bare-headed. Following a Spanish custom, we wore black *mantillas* (black lace head covers which fell down to the shoulders). It was said that the young men watched the women below instead of praying!

Saint-Jean-de-Luz' church beautiful altar, galleries and boat suspended from the ceiling.

Our church is the most beautiful of all Basque region churches. From its high ceiling a fine model of a paddle boat with sails and a steam engine is suspended. It is an *ex-voto* (votive offering or fulfillment of a vow) donated last century by a family from Saint-Jean-de-Luz who brought it back from Newfoundland.

After the bitter winter passed, one of the worst in the twentieth century, April brought around the Easter spring break. Pauline wanted to come home. Her Christmas holiday had been spent sadly away at my stern godmother's house near Pau.

This time she received a French *laissez-passer* (permit) from the Pau's Town Hall to cross over to the occupied zone. When the train arrived at the demarcation line railway check point in Orthez, all passengers had to disembark. Pauline presented her French papers to a very tall, short-cropped grey-haired soldier on duty. She had to really look up to a very impassive face. He briefly glanced at her *laissez-passer* through his thick glasses. One gruff word passed through his thin lips, "*Nein* (no)!"

Pauline tried to ask why, explaining that she was going home. With an abrupt gesture another *nein* was pronounced and she was waved back. She absolutely could not go through! Her only recourse would be to take the train back to Pau. Dejected, feeling very much alone, Pauline returned to the station waiting room. Sitting on a bench waiting for the next train back to Pau, she heard a male voice whisper behind her in French with a German accent, "Don't be afraid and don't turn around."

She was startled, but obeyed the voice's request.

"I heard your story. Write a note to your family, I will mail it for you!"

The man was taking quite a chance! Could she trust him?

"I have nothing to write with," she bravely answered.

"Wait," was the quick response.

A while later, to Pauline's surprise, an older German soldier with a well-worn face and a fatherly smile handed her a sheet of paper and an envelope. He waited patiently while she wrote quickly a brief note explaining to our parents her dilemma. Smiling and without another word, he took the letter to be mailed in the occupied zone. The letter arrived safely. Pauline thought afterward that probably the German soldier may have had a daughter her own age. He had been a kind man.

Pauline took the next train back to Pau where she impatiently waited for Maman's answer.

Monsieur LeBlanc was again contacted by Maman and obtained the name of someone who could help Pauline cross the demarcation line to the occupied zone. When all the arrangements were made Maman called her, "Take the train back to Orthez," Maman instructed her. "At the station you will see a young man with black hair, Jacques, about your age wearing a checkered black and white cap. Smile at him, he will then remove his cap, and take you to his parents' home."

Pauline had no trouble spotting Jacques. They quickly took off, Pauline perched on the top bar of his bicycle. After they had reached his parents' house, Jacques' mother served them a light lunch. The plan was to cross the demarcation line between two patrols. When they arrived at the designated *sentier* (path) it was closed. The only recourse was to cross a small creek. Jacques didn't hesitate. He rolled up his pants, removed his socks and shoes, waded through carrying his bicycle, then came back to get Pauline. As he didn't want her to get wet he picked her up in his arms. Huffing and puffing, Pauline not being light weight, he reached the other side of the creek with his charge. He laughingly said, "It would make a wonderful photo for the papers! A future nun in the arms of a future Protestant pastor! It is too bad that the photo was not taken!" The demarcation line was crossed without a hitch. Pauline was in the occupied zone and shortly after on a train toward home.

In April rationing became harsher, more and more supplies were diverted toward Germany. At Easter time, to the consternation of French children, the traditional chocolate bells eaten with particular gusto were displayed at candy stores windows, but this year made of cardboard. No chocolate!

Rationing swiftly moved down to our feet! In prewar France sixty million shoes were manufactured per year. Part of the 1940 Armistice agreement was that six million pairs of shoes annually would be shipped to Nazi Germany! The French were issued a coupon for their yearly one pair of shoes. Catholic children's parents needed a certificate from their parish priest in order to purchase white shoes for girls' First Communion.

Soon pretty women's shoes were manufactured with wooden wedged soles. I remember one pair, its top was made of multicolored raffia with a beautiful design. I felt taller and elegant! Still I had to get accustomed to walking in this new type of shoes. It was the start of a new feminine silhouette. The wooden shoes clopped noisily against the pavement. The streets had new sounds, definitely distinct from the heavy and noisy Germans' hobnailed boots. After the curfew these shoes became dangerous, they made too much noise! They had to be removed. A song about our wooden shoes was made popular by the well known French singer, Maurice Chevalier. It was titled, *La Symphonie des Semelles en Bois* (The Symphony of the Wooden Soles): "Tap, tap, tap say in the morning the little shoes made of fir...seem to tap dance...it sings life...so good in my heart...comes like a song..."

Coal mines located in northeast France were under German control. Very little reached the French population and even less in our little corner of the world. Still, our conditions were a lot easier, first on account of our temperate climate, and our secret source. THE GERMANS!

In our new quarters the kitchen was located under a terrace. It was very unhealthy as every time it rained, which was often, the walls would sweat. The small coal cooking stove helped somewhat because it was well supplied by a loyal hotel employee. For more than fifteen years, my parents had a handyman named Ignacio who was born in Spain. He was a short, stocky man who could neither read or write, but could fix anything that was broken. I used to be fascinated by his abilities. Before my years at boarding school I would follow him around the hotel and he had taught me how to change the *plombs* of the electric outlets which in France were the equivalents of prewar fuses. As he was very devoted to my parents, Ignacio had stayed in the employ of the Germans. He had told Papa, "I'll keep an eye on the hotel." Cleverly, he found a way to requisition some of the Germans' coal for our use. Amazingly he never got caught.

The hotel coal bin was located on the other side of the back entrance corridor wall of our new lodgings. The walls were of old fragile plaster. Ignacio found a very ingenious way to pass our necessary supply right under the Germans' noses. How? He made a large enough hole in the back corner of the wall. The coal was pushed through the hole. Ignacio would knock at our back door to advise us when we could take our supply. How we smiled putting the coal in the stove!

In that small inconvenient kitchen, Maman produced miracles of cooking. I remember grilled sardines, eaten just with a little bit of salt. Fish also became hard to come by as the fishing fleet could seldom leave the harbor due to the lack of fuel.

People in larger cities were the worst hit, some people were actually starving. Soup kitchens started to be organized. In our little corner of the world we really didn't realize how well off we were!

More, more and more rationing! Less and less food!

Now ration cards were issued for clothing! The textile industry was revolutionized! Synthetic fibers started to appear. Cousin Olga's letters continued to contain amusing stories about life in Paris. She had read in the paper that a French comedian appeared on a stage dressed in a suit too tight for him.

"Latest fashion! Made of tree bark, synthetic, absolutely no wool. One inconvenience is that when it rains, I come home in my underwear!"

A hilarious part of one letter was about her neighbor. He had put his only pair of pants on his balcony to dry. A gust of wind blew them in the street never to be seen again. In protest of the rations he had gone to work in his underwear!

Olga also sent us a disturbing and sad newspaper clipping.

Mangeurs de chats, attention!
(Cat eaters, beware)

"During these days of restrictions, be careful! Cats transmit diseases as their main staple is rats."

A Paris restaurant menu listed, *Fricassé* of alley cat! Olga also mentioned that crows' carcasses were sold for soup. Some Parisians were reduced to eating their pets. Pigeons slowly disappeared from public gardens like the *Tuileries*. Many people were reduced to that point. It was a sad reminder of the long 1870 siege of Paris by the Germans.

Another season of my youth stolen. But buds appeared on trees, no one could stop them. Flowers bloomed. Spring also brought back birds from the south. Birds don't worry about wars and since the occupation they had been safe from avid hunters like Papa and my brother Michel, who could not use their hidden hunting rifles.

During May 1941, one hundred thousand French prisoners of war were released. Payments for maintaining the occupation forces were reduced to 240 million francs a day. This was not done from the goodness of Hitler's heart, but as a gesture of thanks to the Vichy regime for its collaboration, and so the Third Reich would no longer have to feed the prisoners. The remaining prisoners, about a million and a half were kept as pawns, hostages, or forced laborers. This helped release able-bodied Germans to be inducted in the German Armed Forces to conquer Europe for the *Führer's* Nazi regime. Sadly, the remaining prisoners were allowed to receive only two letters a month. This restriction added to their sense of isolation.

June 22, 1941–"Operation Barbarossa"

A date which indirectly was going to change French people's lives in the occupied zone and ours for the better! The *Wehrmacht* invaded Russia with 170 divisions! Many occupation troops left for Germany. By the end of the summer the number of German soldiers billeted in the Basque region was greatly reduced! Those soldiers were needed for the *Wehrmacht's* insatiable hunger at the new ogre–the Eastern Russian front. Slowly the number of soldiers on R & R staying at the hotel, a different sort of soldier from the occupying forces, increased. More were seen relaxing on the beach and in the streets.

The Russian invasion was Hitler's biggest blunder. Hitler had miscalculated the Russian response to his attack on the Soviet Union. Like the Japanese after Pearl Harbor, he was to realize that the supposedly sleeping giant was very much awake. Hitler should have listened to General Rommel, "Know everything about your enemy. It might be the key to his total destruction."

October 1941, was a very sad month for me. Pauline was leaving to start her new life in a religious teaching order. Papa and I accompanied her to Orthez, the town on the imaginary border where we would have to get off the train then return to Saint-Jean-de-Luz. This time she had been able to obtain an *Ausweis*, which were harder and harder to obtain. What a depressing journey, more so for me. We had spent eighteen years together, including six years of boarding school. She was following her calling. I was losing my closest family member. Pauline had been my protector when I, too often, got into trouble either at the convent or with our parents. It was like a part of me was leaving. She had always been the quiet one, studious, and, when young, of a frail nature. I was the opposite, sturdy, vivacious, full of life and mischief. Before Pauline went to present her *Ausweis*, she slowly removed her ivory earrings and handed them to me. After she boarded the train, I cried inside as we had been taught not to show feelings in public.

Maman was more than ever determined to see me married. Despite that fact, I often asked myself, "What am I going to do with my life?" I now would be alone between the two oldest, a twelve-year gap with Michel and the two youngest, and five years with Anne. It was time to fend for myself in new and difficult circumstances. It didn't take me long to realize that now, since I was not going to school, I had a wonderful opportunity to travel and visit Pauline wherever she would be assigned.

Maman was a very intuitive woman blessed with a sixth sense. One day, when she was alone, the doorbell rang. She proceeded toward the front door, drying her hands on her apron. When she opened the door, a tall handsome stranger with a thick head of graying hair and a carefully trimmed mustache was facing her. He was impeccably dressed in a severe looking suit and tie.

"What can I do for you?" she asked.

He answered in fluent French without a trace of an accent, but had neither our *Sud-Ouest* (southwestern) accent or *l'air du pays* (native look), as we would say. All the more reason to be very suspicious of him.

With a pleasant smile he addressed her, "*Madame*, I have been told that you have a daughter who travels to the unoccupied zone and accepts letters from people to post them there. I have some to give her. I am willing to pay very well."

"*Monsieur*," sternly answered Maman, "I am very strict with my daughter. I don't allow her to travel very far. Consequently, she could not be involved in smuggling letters. Good day!"

She slammed the door in his face, a thing that my very proper Maman would have never done before the war. Rude behavior? Perhaps! We were all changing. Maman was not taking chances.

All over France individual protests continued. In Paris, against strict German orders, Parisians continued to deposit flowers on the Unknown Soldier tomb located under the Arch of Triumph.

More posters appeared, saturating our walls and kiosks. The aim was to crack down on the underground.

"Any man helping downed Allied pilots will be shot without trial. Women will be sent to a labor camp."

If you are doing nothing, you are doing wrong.
                                        –Lord Mountbatten

Chapter 7

When sorrows come, they come no single spies, but in battalions.

–King Claudius, Hamlet, Shakespeare

Another season of my youth stolen. The year 1941 was dragging. October brought a hint of the cold temperatures to come. I should have been attending classes at the convent high school in Pau with Pauline. More precious stolen time.

In Saint-Jean-de-Luz like the rest of the occupied zone, supplies were getting harder and harder to secure. In our little corner of France we were not as bad off as the large cities. Each week more than ten thousand head of livestock and tons of butter were requisitioned by the Germans. More and more stores were emptied of their contents. It was a weird sight walking down *rue Gambetta* past store windows emptied of displays.

Papa and Maman were very concerned about our living conditions. After many evenings of deliberations and discussions, they decided that it would be more sensible to move to the country villa, named Menta, *Pausa lekua*

(Peaceful place in Basque). We would be able to grow our own food at our adjoining farm where my brother Michel had started farming in 1940 following his exile by Papa because of his reckless loud comments at the movies about the Germans. Since then, Michel had often urged our parents to move to the countryside. Before the occupation no major decisions had been discussed in front of the younger Branquet children. Now living for the first time as a family in close quarters, important decisions were discussed openly.

At my age I had an insatiable appetite, and my younger siblings needed good food for their growth. After many evenings of soul searching they followed Michel's advice. At least there we would have enough to eat.

Late fall 1941 we moved to Olhette where the villa was located. It was five kilometers from Saint-Jean-de-Luz, the

Villa in its present state.

last three on steep hills. The half mile leading to the villa was an unpaved, narrow, winding trail between thick hedges of blackberry bushes. The succulent blackberries, gathered despite the thorns, would become a welcome addition to our diet. They left violet hands and exquisite taste in our mouths. The trail was very hard on my bicycle and me. I took quite a few brutal falls, the worst when I flew over the handlebars, the front wheel having hit a rock.

The villa was built on a little hill, the surrounding landscape dotted with scattered Basque style white-washed farms, with red tiled roofs, one side longer than the other all facing east toward the rising sun. The facades had spaced wooden partitions painted in lively colors. Some looked niched in the rolling hills and mountains. Compared to the farms, the villa was an impressive structure, three stories high with dormers. The front bedrooms had a balcony the width of the house from which passion flowers, wisteria, and green creeping vines clung. The neighboring Basque farmers called the villa, *le Château* (the castle).

The villa had been designed and built by Maman's eldest brother, Henri, a contractor. The ground floor consisted of a dining room, a large living room with a fireplace and an adjoining small cozy sitting room-library with comfy chairs made for reading. The old fashioned bookcase with intricate ornamental *grille* (latticed) doors housed Papa's books hidden by flowered curtains. The large kitchen behind the dining room had a large fireplace and a pantry. In the fireplace the fire was always lit or smoldering. During the winter we didn't use the unheated dining room. Our meals were eaten in the warm kitchen which had a Basque style breakfront full of beautiful old dishes. I soon learned to chop wood for the kitchen with an ax. All ground floor rooms had beamed ceilings.

The second floor was reached by a carpeted staircase. In summers, its landing was at times used as a theater. The performances are locked in the midst of my mind. One antic was sliding down the banister and breaking its decorated end. More scolding from Maman! She was despairing at having a seventeen-year old fearless tomboy. How would she be able to marry me to one of the stuffy older eligible men in town which she had her heart set on! Was I, in a subconscious way, rebelling against her desire to choose my husband without consulting me?

The second floor landing led to a large corridor flanked by two bedrooms on each side and a bathroom. The third floor consisted of two servants' bedrooms, and an attic. All very roomy.

I slept in one of the front bedrooms alone. During their vacations Jean had his own room and Anne, then age twelve, shared mine. Gone was my privacy. In winter I left the windows opened. Why not! Same temperature inside or out. It was sheer torture getting dressed in the morning. The secret was to fold one's clothes that were going to be worn the following day and put them under the covers at the end of the bed. My body heat kept them warm. In the morning, the other secret was to get dressed under the covers. I became very adept at it. Baths were taken in the evening.

Electricity had not as yet reached that very remote area of the Pyrénées, but the villa had running water heated by the kitchen stove. A heating system had not been installed because the villa had been used only as a summer residence.

For all of us the villa became a refuge, a cocoon and, for me, a peaceful place. We felt that no *sale Boche* (dirty Kraut) would soil its floor with their boots. There were many days that it was easy for me to forget that a lot of sadness existed beyond my little corner of the world.

The villa and its surroundings gave a picture of freshness and gaiety. It was surrounded by beautiful sloped ground, *au naturel* (not landscaped). It made a vivid blot in the heart of multitudes of tall trees which grew so freely in that fertile soil. As an amateur horticulturist, over the years Papa had planted all sorts of unusual trees. He was also very proud of his attempts at grafting.

We settled into country life, which was foreign to my parents. Their adjustment was hard. It was quite a strange sight watching my parents work at farming, especially Maman with her formerly manicured hands on her knees in the garden planting, weeding or picking vegetables for our meals. Her manicurist had come weekly to the hotel. Now her hair, once with a hint of weave done with a curling iron was now severely pulled back in a chignon. My impeccably dressed Papa now wore old clothes, a black Basque *béret*, creased into a peak perched on his head and his ever present cigarette between his lips. No more spats on his shoes. What a contrast!

Having an immense love of outdoor life, I was in my element. Seven summers had been spent at the villa with *Mademoiselle* Durcudoy and my siblings. Again, many of the chores fell upon my shoulders. Like most teenagers, I resented it. I was at the wrong age for escaping duties like the younger children. Anne and Jean were at the villa only during their vacations and when home disappeared at chore time. And they always got away with it.

My clothes were the same as during our summer vacations. They had been made by the hotel linen maid who was also a seamstress. During the occupation I didn't get a chance to acquire new clothes like most teenagers love to.

No more chefs, waiters, maids, handyman! Both Maman and Papa turned out to be good cooks. Another weird sight was Maman killing chickens. Basque women are very adaptable, a trait that I have inherited. Now that I was getting to know my parents, I greatly admired them even though I didn't get along with Maman, probably because we were so much alike.

No more chauffeur, Papa driving our private car! For the adults and younger siblings, the mode of transportation would be horse and buggy. At the farm we had an old mare, Rosalie, who despite her slow nature would get the family back and forth to Saint-Jean-de-Luz. As for many other French people my mode of transportation was a bicycle.

Constant use on difficult paths was hard on my bicycle. Due to the scarcity of inner tubes, I had to learn to repair mine. It became a constant worry. When the time came, I made a big production of it. First, I fetched a pan of water, then turned the bicycle upside down, removed tires and inner tubes. I would then pump air into the inner tube and slowly dipped it in the water until bubbles showed where the repairs were needed. After the hole, or more often holes, were located, the tube had to be dried. Using a special scraper, I smoothed the area where the holes were found, then glued on small patches. The bicycle was reassembled hoping that the repairs would hold. Over the years it became routine. Used repaired tires could be purchased at the bicycle shop. For a teenager all these new experiences were a challenge. I was becoming more and more self-reliant.

Summertime cherries abounded, one particular cherry tree was at the bottom of a steep ravine. Papa, very conservatively used a ladder to gather them. As usual I had climbed the tree like a monkey. All of a sudden I heard Papa scream, "Maita, help! The ladder fell!"

He made such a sight, hanging from a limb that I burst out laughing. Some choice words followed. I was hearing my Papa using more often a different kind of language! I scrambled down, went to his rescue by putting the ladder under him. Papa was saved! Later I bombarded him with pits of eaten cherries. What could he do? We both laughed. We all surely needed to find little pleasures in daily living!

We grew most of our food. During one of his trips to town Papa purchased, with our ration cards, five kilos of dried beans. Maman was delighted, but she later discovered that they were infested by weevils. After being thoroughly boiled the dead beasties floated to the top and Maman scooped them out. Even so it was hard eating the beans without thinking of their former tenants! I could imagine some of them floating in my stomach. It took me decades before I could eat beans comfortably.

We also grew rutabaga. Oh, how I hated their sweetish taste! Maman prepared them in all sorts of different ways, with tomatoes, pimentos, fried or boiled, still they were always distasteful. We were eating cattle feed. Eating Jerusalem artichokes was like a penance to me.

Sometimes when Maman went to town with the buggy she would ask me to go with her. I really didn't like it because Rosalie was so slow, clop, clop. I preferred the freedom and speed of my bicycle. On a particular trip, after we reached the main road leading to Saint-Jean-de-Luz, we slowly passed a German soldier walking on the side of the road. Without a word he jumped on the back of the open carriage. We could not object to his hitchhiking. Calmly, Maman, without missing a word of our conversation, kept on driving. She didn't acknowledge his presence. When we arrived in town, silently he jumped out. We had barely seen the back of his *verdigris* uniform, not even seen his face or heard his voice. It was a strange experience!

Cousin Olga had a brother Charles who was the owner of a beauty salon in Paris. That summer he sent his two children, Felix fourteen and Solange twelve, to spend the summer with us at the villa where they would have enough to eat. Parisians kids, they had never seen or lived on a farm. Everything was a discovery. They were given my room and I moved to the attic domestics' room where, when on vacation, my little sister Anne joined me. I enjoyed the room on the third floor and chose to remain high above the family. It gave me more privacy.

Summer thunderstorms were frequent. Through the open window I could see the splitting, jagged fragments of lightning. It was a beautiful sight. The thunder sounded louder due to the proximity of the mountains. The storms were always of short duration and often followed by rain. Anne hated thunder. During the storms, her trembling voice would call softly, "Maita, can I come to your bed?"

The answer would always be yes. In the dark, her small feet would scurry over the parquet floor, her white nightgown flying around like angel wings. Wordlessly, she would cuddle next to me and soon be fast asleep. Five decades later Anne admits that she still hates thunderstorms, but she can't come to my bed. We are now 6000 miles apart.

Papa, an avid reader, had a thirst for knowledge that was passed on to me. He left me a great legacy, curiosity about everything and a passion for books. At the villa he had quite a collection of interesting and fascinating, mostly non-fiction, books like translations of Jack London's writings. I would sneak books to my room and hide them under the mattress because Maman wanted to screen my reading material. During the day there were too many chores—no time for reading, except during *sieste* (afternoon nap) time. Some evenings I would read in bed, wasting the candles which were so hard to come by. Maman would measure my reading time by the length of my candles like one does with an alcoholic's bottle. Little lies would follow, "I fell asleep without putting the candle out!" I am sure she didn't believe a word, or did she? These books read on the sly became spurs to my runaway imagination. I dreamt of faraway countries.

For some unknown reason, the game of Monopoly was impossible to find for sale in the stores. Why? A mystery! Was it a German ploy to stop children from dealing with the sale of expensive French pieces of property, *Rue de la Paix* in Paris? Messing up their grand plans for Europe? That didn't stop me. Even though paper was scarce I made up a game. It had been difficult to find enough paper of the same color for the money. When I designed the board, my unknown artistic talents started to show. We had many, many summer evenings of laughter buying and selling French real estate on the Riviera or in Paris, a city which, due to the occupation, I had not as yet seen. As candles were not easily found for purchase carbide lamps were used. How messy they were! During our endless Monopoly or card games, our blackened faces added to our laughter. We looked like coal miners.

During the years passed at the villa I learned many things, except cooking which later became quite a disadvantage. Another assigned chore was cheese making. In the basement we had hanging latticed shelves covered with straw where new cheeses were laid. Every other day I went down with a pail of water and a clean cloth. The cheese had to be washed, dried, and turned over. This process would develop their external coating. I became quite a cheese maker. A real boring chore was butter churning by hand, it seemed to take so long. Sitting in one place for any length of time for me had always been a hardship!

Before the occupation we never had done our own laundry. The hotel linens had been professionally laundered, our personal clothes washed by a maid. It became quite a production, and so little soap was available for purchase. Eventually we had to make our own. A formula had been found consisting of a mixture of caustic soda, beef grease and resin. At the farm it was not a problem, we had all the ingredients.

I did the wash because Maman was too busy with cooking or gardening. I washed at an outdoor cement washboard, scrubbed and rinsed. It was hard, the wet sheets were heavy. I spread them overnight on the grass, because the dew was supposed to whiten them. Personal clothing was spread on bushes. Another chore I didn't favor during our stay at the villa was the ironing. It was done with old fashioned irons heated in front of the fireplace. Summertime those jobs were overwhelming with everyone on vacation and still no help.

Papa and my brother Michel were heavy smokers, their brand of cigarettes, strong grey tobacco, *les Gauloises.* They were now rationed, getting more scarce and expensive. Papa's average consumption was at least one pack a day. "Two packs a month only," Papa one day exploded "and only if the packing boxes are returned!" He decided to grow their tobacco supply between the corn stalks grown in France for chicken feed only. It was strictly *verboten* by the Germans as, it seemed, a million other things. But they had better things to do than inspect far away farms! After Papa picked the tobacco leaves, he hung them to dry on cords which he had previously strung wall to wall in the living room. After drying came the cutting process. Maman's exasperated voice would often be heard, "Louis, don't use my good kitchen knives to cut your smelly tobacco!"

Most of the time Papa would say that he had not heard her. During World War I he had served as a male nurse in a field army hospital located near the trenches at the front in northeastern France. His hearing had been damaged by a bomb which had exploded nearby. Over the years, Maman always said that he had selective hearing. When it came to the tobacco, Papa's supposed deafness and addiction won the battle. He became totally deaf.

About two kilometers away from the villa we could see Maman's younger brother *Tonton* (familiar term for uncle) Joseph's farm. He had four children. The eldest, Pasco, was my age. *Tonton* Joseph was our favorite uncle, a jolly short man with a hawkish face weathered by years lived on a farm, and gnarled hands, work worn from hard work. When he smiled his face would crinkle. *Tonton* was never seen indoors or outdoors without his Basque *béret* and a cigarette in his mouth. I had always been fascinated by his way of rolling his own cigarettes. It was quite a ritual. First the tobacco pouch would appear from his shirt pocket together with a package of thin cigarette paper. Delicately one sheet would be pulled and curled to receive the tobacco which he spread evenly. His technique was perfect, just the right amount of tobacco, carefully rolled and then the paper licked to seal it. The tobacco pouch strings were pulled shut with his teeth for the pouch to disappear back in his shirt pocket.

Tonton's farm, Marticott, had a large apple orchard and every year he made delicious *sagarnoa* (cider in Basque) which is the national Basque drink. At times he would let us mash the apples with our bare feet in a special area. That was fun!

When Pasco and I were not being kept busy by our parents, we spent our rare spare time together. When we had moved to the villa I had lost my playmate, cousin Léon. Pasco and I had often discussed the possibility of smoking. We thought it would make us feel grown up. We wanted to try what so many of our older male relatives seemed to enjoy so much. Women we knew never smoked. It would be a daring thing to do without being caught for taking some of Papa's home grown tobacco supply. Where could we do it? We opted for the corn field. It would give us ample cover. Pasco had taken a couple of sheets of his father's cigarette paper. He rolled the cigarettes like he had seen his father do for many years. I delicately and elegantly held my cigarette the way I had seen the hotel clients do. I felt so glamorous sitting in the corn field and so grown up! After a session of giggling, we started puffing. It didn't take long for both of us to turn green and get sick to our stomachs. It was the last time we tried that experiment.

Papa went to town regularly to bring supplies to my older sister Marie. He would also check the apartment and pick up the mail. The mailman didn't make deliveries in our remote, little corner of the world at the foot of the Pyrénées. Papa also often visited his long time barber, Marcel, for a haircut or to listen to the town's gossip. One time Marcel mentioned a new decree that effected him. Beauty salons and barber shops had to salvage the cut hair. The whole of occupied France had to furnish 200 metric tons per month!

On a fall breezy day, Michel and I were plowing a field. At Basque farms plowing is done in a very different way from the rest of France. The fields are on steep inclines, two pairs of cows are used, one pair down and two going up. Midway up the hill I screamed, "Michel, stop!"

Near a furrow, I had sighted some baby rabbits. We had a heated argument which was usual with him. Our twelve-year age difference had always created many problems. To him I was just a kid and he was often very mean. We didn't get along. I wanted to keep and care for the baby rabbits. Michel insisted that they would die without their mother. I was adamant. "I will ask Maman," I angrily retorted running toward the villa leaving him in the middle of the field. My words were convincing. I told her, "They multiply fast, eventually they will add variety to our daily diet."

How happy I was with my little rabbits that I could care for. They became my babies. Everyday, I lovingly fed them cow's milk and they thrived in the rabbit bassinet that I had made of pieces of an old blanket and grass. As they grew Papa decided to build a coop to house them. It was quite a chore for poor inexperienced Papa. In their new home, my little family grew and multiplied. It became my responsibility to feed them and later the descendants of my early rabbits. What a windfall to our diet it turned out to be to have nurtured those wild rabbits.

VERBOTEN again!

Verboten to butcher livestock without permission from the German authorities. Who was going to ask them? Surely not us! It was impossible for the occupation forces to keep track of the small farms' cows, pigs or sheep. How would they ever find out if someone did some butchering? We didn't worry about our neighbors because the Basques are very closed mouthed, even had they been close enough to see what we did.

One chilly December day Pasco and I came across a dead sheep. It was later discovered that it had been mauled by our farm dog. *Tonton* Joseph was consulted. "Destroy it! Once they eat sheep meat, they acquire a taste for it," he declared.

It was a sad occasion as we all liked our dog. It fell upon Michel to do the killing. After the dog's death, it was decided, with my two younger siblings on holiday, that the dog deserved a proper burial. I found a perfect spot under an oak tree in a corner of the villa's extended grounds.

As we didn't have a refrigerator, the sheep had to be butchered immediately. Meat was too scarce to be wasted. We never knew that so many emergencies could happen on a farm. We soon realized that country life never had a dull moment. Naturally Papa didn't go to town to get permission from the German authorities to keep the sheep.

In the midst of the butchering, my younger brother Jean all of a sudden came in screaming. Out of breath he was barely able to say, "*Un Boche au portail! Un Boche au portail* (A Kraut at the gate)!*"

My younger siblings and I had good lungs, good screamers which we had never been able to test before the war. During the occupation, many genteel manners went by the wayside.

"What are we going to do?" asked Michel.

Killing domestic animals without the Germans' permission was now *VERBOTEN*, and punishable by heavy fines. They would never believe that a dog had done the job for us. None of us knew if the German was alone, armed or what he wanted. A quick decision was made by Maman, she quickly ordered, "Maita, go to bed. Michel wrap the lamb in a lot of newspapers, put it next to her. Everybody else clean up in a hurry."

Oh, yuck! A dead lamb next to me under the covers. Well, it would be food! Maman felt that if the German soldier wanted to inspect the second floor, she would tell them that I was quarantined with the measles. Fortunately, it was a false alarm. The German was another rare, lost soldier just passing by, probably looking for a farm where he could buy food. He had not even come on the property. Case of the jitters. It seemed that I could be counted on in time of emergencies! This one was kind of messy!

Daily, Maman sent me to gather eggs. Since we were living in the country we had taken the habit of eating the Basque breakfast of *arolxia eta xingarra* (Basque for smoked ham and eggs). One day, I left swinging the basket, whistling happily once out of Maman's earshot. Even in the country she frowned on whistling. It is not ladylike, she would admonish. When I arrived in the farmyard, the tawny hens were pecking and strutting with the rooster proudly parading among them. As I was gathering the eggs I heard behind me the chickens cackling and noisily scattering. I turned around to check the commotion. A young, blond smooth-cheeked German soldier of average height, with a toothy grin, seemingly not much older than I, was standing in the courtyard. He had taken me totally by surprise. The soldier took a few steps toward me pointing at the basket. From the bottom of my lungs I let out a piercing scream, "Papa, Michel, *au secours* (help)!"

At the same time, I purposely threw the basket on the ground, smashing all the eggs into a yellow gooey mess. Better break them than sell or give them to a *Boche*. Papa arrived out of breath, followed shortly by Michel. Papa simply told the soldier, "*raus* (go away)."

The soldier was so startled by the whole incident that without uttering a word he turned around and left. Papa and Michel could have used their well-hidden hunting riffles, but disappearances of soldiers were brutally punished by retaliations on the male population of the area. So far it had not happened in our little corner of the world.

The rifles stayed hidden in the old hollow oak tree. The soldier had not looked armed and probably was just hungry. Léon and I had once seen from our city apartment windows overlooking the park a German soup kitchen. What was ladled resembled very thin broth. We had commented to each other that we ate better than the *Boches*.

One cold fall Sunday the family went to Mass at the picturesque little old church of Urrugne. Basque villages are centered around their churches most of which have a clock tower. This church had a sun dial with a very interesting Latin annotation: *Vulnerant omnes, ultima necat* (All wound, the last one kills).

The church of Urrugne was a one-hour walking distance from the villa through fields and on ill defined paths. Next to the church, as one can always find at Basque churches, the free-standing wall of the *fronton* (ball court) where games were played mostly after high Mass. On Sundays, the family would be gone for at least four hours from home. The Basque pastor was long winded like my godfather. Michel had left the previous night stating that he was visiting a farmer closer to the mountains. Without explanation he would often mysteriously disappear for a couple days. I was left behind to keep an eye on the villa and farm. I would go alone to a later Mass.

Before leaving Michel had asked me to check the stable, a cow was due to give birth. Mid-morning I leisurely walked to the farm to look into the stable. To my consternation the cow was in labor. What to do? Michel had not left any instructions. I ran to the closest neighboring farm for advice. I found Martin in his courtyard. He had the typical

Basque chiseled face with a sharp, long nose and strong chin. His *béret* was perched on his head. He was rolling a cigarette. Out of breath I explained the situation. Calmly, he told me, "Let the cow do her job. When the calf is born, rub it with straw and give some wine to the mother."

Oh, how gross! I thought. I could not believe that I had to do that dirty work! Wine to the cow, he must be crazy! Nevertheless in my total ignorance I followed his instructions, never realizing that he was pulling my leg. How he must have laughed at us, his city folks neighbors. After all, I had been brought up in a sterile environment, and at seventeen it was my first exposure to the birthing process. Surprisingly the mother loved her wine! I could have sworn that she gave me a cow's smile! The wine, I decided was a token of our thanks for bringing into the world valuable future meals. *Merci, Madame* Cow. When my parents returned they could not believe that I had trusted Martin. Teasing from the whole family lasted many weeks.

As city folks, neither Papa or Michel knew how to cut hay with a long handled sickle, a very tricky task. *Tonton* Joseph was a master at it. As usual he was available to help. His graceful rhythm was a sight to behold. Every so often he would stop to sharpen the blade. Attached to his belt was a wooden container which held water and the stone which sharpened the sickle blade.

The following day, Papa, Michel and I had to turn the hay for the drying process with wooden handmade hay-rakes. Hard work! How we watched daily the sky for signs of storms. We never knew whether those puffy clouds would bring rain. Like all farmers, we were at the mercy of the elements. When the hay was dry, Michel and I had to fork it onto a cart pulled by two cows. The hardest part for me was forking it up to Michel from the cart to the loft where he was on the receiving end. The rest ended on hay stacks. Very hard work for a growing five-foot-four-inch city teenager who had never done that kind of work. No one else was there to do it.

Wheat harvesting was another problem. We had to borrow a threshing machine from a neighboring farmer. Again no one knew how to use it. Always *Tonton* was there to the rescue, my parents relied on him so much.

At the villa, in our little corner of the world, we were leading a relatively peaceful life. That winter, I became very sick. It had started with headaches, sluggishness which was rare with me, no one made much of it including myself. One morning I could not get up. Maman had called me several times, not receiving an answer she came up to my bedroom. I was burning with a high fever, my eyes were sunk deep in their sockets, each breathe was an effort to bring air into my lungs. Maman called Papa. They were frightened, thinking that I would die. It was the first and only time that I saw them together at my bedside looking at me. How often I had craved their affection which they had not been able to give me.

Papa took the buggy to fetch Dr. Blazy in Saint-Jean-de-Luz. His diagnosis—diphtheria, a very uncommon, dreadful sickness. The serum had to be secured from the hospital in Ciboure. Another trip had to be made to the city. Thirty anxious hours were to pass before knowing whether I would survive. With my robust Basque heritage and the serum, I was able to recover or was it because, my secret love, Dr. Blazy had been at my bedside?

As our meat supply was getting low, Papa decided that
an old Jersey milking cow that we had named Cunégonde
(Empress Kunigunde, wife of Henry II of Germany, elev-
enth century) was going to be slaughtered. She was no
longer able to produce much milk. We took her photograph.
How sad we were! Michel was appointed the butcher, but
he had no idea how to proceed. City upbringing had not
prepared him for all these farmer's duties. Our closest
neighbor, Martin, agreed to help. Again, we naturally had
not asked permission from the Germans to butcher.

Then came the time to kill our biggest pig. Again we
took photographs of our fat pig. *Tonton* and his wife
Catherine came to help. She was a typical Basque woman,
short and portly, her graying hair sternly combed back from
her face in nondescript waves ending in a chignon. In the
farm's kitchen the long table took most of the room and
was scrubbed with a brush. Basins were filed with boiling
water. On the table knives of many sizes were aligned,
condiments of all sorts, and pounds of coarse salt set near
by. *Tonton* like a symphony director waved the largest knife.
The ceremony was started and well orchestrated. Short
sentences would fly from one person to another, "Pass me
the salt. Get me more hot water."

I watched a short while and left. I didn't like that gory
sight. But later, I didn't refuse to eat the delicious bacon,
ham, pork chops or other good meat from the pig. Hams
were hung from the villa's beamed kitchen ceiling to be
slowly smoked from the fireplace smoke. Our meat supply
would last quite a while.

Life on the farm isolated me from contact with people
my own age except my cousin Pasco. It turned out to be

quite a handicap. I was not given the chance to form the necessary close female friendships, and it left me without an anchor. Maman and I had a hard time communicating, after all during the ten years previous to the occupation I had rarely seen her. It is hard to believe that I could not ever ask her about the facts of life.

The occupation also meant I didn't have appropriate recreation. For me, time was on hold, and the result was loss of my teenage years. The continuity of growing up was broken never to be connected again. I was living in a closed, unusually isolated and protected world. I felt stifled in that unique environment and rebelled more strongly than most teenagers need to. Those stolen years left an indelible mark which would effect me for all the years to come. The customary pre-war way of life for teenagers was foreign to me. I saw some friends my own age in town, but on rare occasions. During the occupation most French women endured one way or another in that artificial life and teenagers were no exception.

In December 1941, a notorious German decree from General Keitel.

"French citizens found guilty of criminal acts against the Reich will be arrested to disappear without a trace."

Nice way of ending the year!

In our little corner of the world, days, weeks and months passed without signs of relief from escalating problems with the occupation forces. Chances of resuming my education looked bleak. More stolen years!

To know how to live is to know enough.
                                            –Old Basque saying

Chapter 8

Wer alles defendiersen will, defendieret gar nicht.
(Who wants to defend all, defends nothing.)

-*Frederick the Great*

One does not defend a country with walls, nor its
inhabitants with ditches.

-*Sultan of Baybars to the Jerusalem Saint Jean Hospitalliers who
were defending the Tower of Arsouf against the Mamelouks in 1265*

August 1942, Hitler gave the order to start the construction of *Festung Europa* (Fortress of Europe). He should have taken counsel from history.

Fritz Todt, a German civil engineer was the creator/designer of the *Atlantikwall* (Atlantic wall). It was built to prevent an invasion from the Allies. After Todt's death in a plane crash, Albert Speer became the Director of the Todt Organization.

The construction was started along the western coast of Europe from Holland to Belgium and then along France's Atlantic coast to the Spanish border. In Saint-Jean-de-Luz bunkers and blockhouses were built into the rock on both sides of the bay. They later were painted like houses with fake windows and curtains. Access roads to these areas were closed with barbed wire and big signs in two languages posted:

VERBOTEN

DÉFENSE DE PASSER (no trespassing)

In Ciboure, the sister city across the river, twenty-four German officers, ninety-eight warrant officers and 437 soldiers were billeted to work on the wall. As time passed more and more local French workers were drafted by the Germans to relieve the soldiers who were badly needed at the Russian front. Eventually only one officer was left to supervise 250 French workers who continued the building of the wall. Cannons were installed on both sides of the river Nivelle which ends in the harbor. It is recorded that French workers didn't work very hard, often reporting late for work and some often quite drunk.

On a regular basis the Résistance sent information on the progress of the building of the wall to England. The construction was never completed, but by June, 1944 the *Atlantikwall* stretched two thousand kilometers. It needed to be guarded night and day by the *Wehrmacht*. Eventually five hundred thousand soldiers were assigned to that duty. The bunkers were equipped with anti-aircraft guns. It was declared by the Third Reich to be an impassable wall!

After the Christmas holiday Pauline, returning to the convent school without an *Ausweis*, had another adventure. To join our cousin Pascal she had taken a different route. He was also traveling to the unoccupied zone without a permit. It took them three long days to reach Pau. At the demarcation line they had to crawl noiselessly behind a hedge because the *Feldgendarmerie* was patrolling on the other side of the hedge. They finally made it to the unoccupied zone walking carefully on the icy road, but new troubles had nearly overwhelmed them. At the bus depot, French soldiers were milling around, and advised them that the last bus for Pau had already departed! Without kindness one said, "It is typical of the Basques to travel this way!" Sarcastically another one added, "Especially a woman!"

Pauline and Pascal had not expected that kind of treatment from their countrymen. What could they do?

Bravely they tied their suitcases on their backs with scarfs, and started to walk. A friend's house was still ten kilometers away. They had to be careful, some parts of the road were icy. It was all right for a while, but their feet were wet, they were hungry. In a little village they stopped at a cafe to drink a horrible ersatz coffee, but it was warm! Not being in possession of their ration cards they could not even buy some bread. Off again! To give each other courage they sang an old marching song,

Un kilomètre à pied ça use, ça use, un kilomètre à pied ça use les souliers. (One kilometer on foot, wears, wears, one kilometer on foot wears out shoes.) The song's verses repeated, counting from one kilometer to two and on and on.

Naturally, due to the lack of fuel, no cars were in sight for hitchhiking. Finally they arrived, exhausted and soaked. They were so grateful to be in a house where they could change into dry clothes, eat and then sleep in a nice bed. The following day, Pauline and Pascal were able to catch a bus for Pau. What an ordeal!

From England, then Algeria, *Général de Gaulle* exhorted his countrymen and women to work toward their own liberation.

"The flame of French resistance must not and shall not be extinguished!"

Communications by the underground with England were made with radios which had been air dropped. The Résistance gathered information about the Germans' military activities and advised names of escapees who made it to freedom. Their networks kept on expanding and growing. They were very well organized for guerrilla warfare and harassment. France was the most heavily populated and industrialized of the six other occupied countries. It had a well-developed railroad system against which saboteurs reaped their richest harvest. Trains and railway stations were under constant attack, disrupting German movement of troops, war material and supplies. French people could no longer count on reliable train schedules for their only mode of long distance transportation. Acts of sabotage included nails spread on roads, and stealing the *Wehrmacht's* horses, really taking back requisitioned French horses.

Tension was running high between the occupying forces and the population. Boldly but still on the sly, many ordinary French people like Pauline and I went out of their way to annoy and insult the troops in very subtle ways. People who spoke German and were asked directions by a soldier would either shrug their shoulders, walk away or point in the wrong direction. The Germans didn't know how to deal with these intractable French people. Many bartenders, especially in the north, feigned ignorance and listened to the soldiers conversations, gleaning military information. It was a form of refusal to submit, a way to keep hope alive. Like many other French people, we continued to show our patriotism in as many small ways as we could. We seized on every little way to annoy the Germans.

Cousin Olga had written about another elderly French-woman in Paris who crossed the *Champs-Elysées* leaning on her cane interrupting a German military parade. She was escorted to the other side by an officer. She had disrupted *ordnung* (order).

Since the beginning of the occupation the Basque region had been spared any violence. The first incident happened when an English torpedo boat fired on the coastal town of Bidart, five kilometers north of Saint-Jean-de-Luz. Small damage was reported to a school and a villa. The *Kreigsma-rine* (German Navy) fired back missing their target. The British ship left unscathed. Following that incident nets were dropped at the entrances of the natural harbors on the Basque coast, Saint-Jean-de-Luz and Bayonne. Artillery batteries were installed along the Basque coast. Later an-other British Air Force Lancaster was downed in the Atlantic, five bodies were recovered. A well-attended fu-neral Mass by the *Luziens* was said at our Catholic Church followed by burial at the local cemetery. Flowers were often secretly deposited on the tombstones.

Without the world's knowledge, and least ours, Hitler had special plans for France. Dr. Paul Joseph Goebbels, Nazi Propaganda Minister, had made the following state-ment at a *Wehrmacht* High Command meeting: "If the French knew what the *Führer* intends to extract from them, it is probable that their eyes would go out of their heads."

Hitler planned to turn France into an agricultural country to feed his Aryan race. The enslaved country would be used for the pleasure of their masters. As if such a plan was not bad enough, Goebbels added, "If they don't cooperate, we will destroy France and bring her to her knees."

Dreadful orders for France: *Gauleiter* (German Military Governor) Fritz Sauckel was ordered by Hitler to draft workers from all occupied countries. They were needed to work in the Reich factories to relieve able-bodied Germans for the insatiable ogre—the *Wehrmacht!* On the Russian front many Germans were dying fighting for Hitler's follies. More soldiers were needed. Sauckel tried to seduce Frenchmen with promises of high wages. He became the slave trader of the occupied countries.

France had a quota of two hundred fifty thousand workers. In Vichy, seat of the puppet Nazi-controlled French regime, Premier Pierre Laval compromised. One French prisoner of war to be liberated in exchange for three workers leaving for the Reich factories. To justify himself he declared, "I wish a German victory because otherwise Bolshevism will conquer Europe."

It was simple blackmail. The first liberated prisoners arrived near Paris August 11, 1942. It was declared a kind gesture from the *Führer!*

Premier Pierre Laval had agreed to induct French laborers for the benefit of Third Reich industries, herding free men into what amounted to penal servitude. His other excuse was that it was taking the place of obligatory drafting of young Frenchmen.

On the radio, Pierre Laval addressed workers, "Workers of France!... We have a lot of unemployment...Germany is in dire need of you! It is to liberate French prisoners that you are going to work in Germany...It is also for your country, to enable France to find its place in the Europe of tomorrow. That is why you are going to answer my call."

Papa, reading Laval's speech in the newspaper, exploded. A roar came from his armchair, "That rotten Laval! He wishes the Germans' victory. He should be hanged!" Crumpling the paper, throwing it across the room in disgust, he angrily stomped out of the room!

The American government notified Vichy that sending French manpower to Germany constituted aid to the enemy.

Many posters were pasted glorifying work in Germany. One showed a smiling Frenchman holding an electric drill.

"Work in Germany is not deportation"

"*Je travaille en Allemagne* (I work in Germany)
Pour la relève (For the release)
Pour ma famille (For my family)
Pour la France (For France).

Another showed a young woman holding a child in her arms with a background of workingmen with the caption:

"*Finis les mauvais jours.*
Papa gagne de l'argent en Allemagne!
(Gone are the bad days.
Daddy earns money in Germany!)"

Besides inundation by posters and newspaper articles, Vichy radio broadcasts declared that, "To work in Germany is earning a living under good conditions, see for yourself." It later was revealed to be virtual slavery under very harsh conditions.

To the consternation of his parents, a first cousin Pierre, who lived in Orègue, Maman's hometown, was drafted to work in Germany. He was twenty years old. His letters confirmed the sad fact that like other unwilling young men from different countries he was suffering from overwork, poor nutrition and homesickness. Pierre had never been away from his village. Like my brother-in-law Paul when he returned after the war, he was in very poor health and remained so. Pierre is now deceased from the results of those years of servitude and forced labor.

Rumors often overshadowed the truth, they seemed never ending. Sauckel was not looking as yet to recruit students or women as they would not make the best of workers. The Reich so far needed trained, specialized factory workers.

It didn't take long for Sauckel to decree that ALL men and women living in German occupied countries were liable to be drafted to work in Germany. Would I have to escape to Spain like the men? I was very worried. Some rumors were scary, saying that the Nazis were using women as prostitutes. Soon after, a rumor circulated that women would be drafted unless they were students. August 10, I was going to turn eighteen. Could that awful fate happen to me? I felt in great danger. The threat was getting too close. For a while, my preoccupation overshadowed my usual sunny personality. Of all my siblings I was the only who could possibly be drafted. My parents shared my grave concerns. Pauline didn't have to worry, she had her new life planned in a convent.

As a shield I was enrolled in the closest university in Bordeaux, 200 kilometers away. Not having a high school diploma, my selection of courses was very limited. I enrolled in a law course which after graduation would enable me to work as a clerk in a notary's office. In France, notaries draw wills, real estate and marriage contracts, but aren't counselors in legal cases. The long commuting and stress were endured as a necessity. Anything rather than be drafted and work for the *sales Boches* (dirty Krauts). It was hard studying after those long trips. In the French terminology, I was going up to Bordeaux (north) and down (south) as though the city was on top of a mountain and I lived in a valley!

Premier Laval declared the creation of S.T.O. *Service de Travail Obligatoire*, (Compulsory Work, like Military service) for young men for a two-year duration. Farmers were exempted as they were needed to grow food for the Third Reich. These men had no choice unless they found their way to the underground or to Spain. Without knowing it Laval and Hitler became the best suppliers of the Résistance. The young men who joined the Résistance were supplied with false identification cards and weapons.

All over France, protests were staged against the drafting of young French men and women. They were crushed by the Germans.

Monsignor Vansteenberghe, Catholic bishop of our region from the Bayonne Cathedral's pulpit expressed his strong opposition to the drafting of French workers. The

Bayonne Kommandant requested his resignation. It was not granted! The Germans could not lock horns with the Catholic Church and its millions of French followers. Reprisals against a member of the clergy in that part of France could have caused a lot of problems with the Basques. The Germans could not afford a rebellion. They were already spread out too thin.

By September, only fifty thousand Frenchmen, a small part of the ordered workers, had left for Germany. Sauckel was ordered to double his efforts. Manpower was badly needed. In Vichy, Laval requested that French law control the drafting of the workers. The French National Department of Employment declared that men between the ages of eighteen and fifty, single women twenty-one to thirty-five would have to do any kind of work the government would judge beneficial to the nation. They would have to remain available. My age, eighteen, so far would save me from this awful fate! Several Vichy-French ministers had the courage to criticize that decision declaring, "We don't have the right to enslave ourselves."

In September the USAF destroyed the very strategic French railroad sidings of Rouen. Unfortunately some bombs fell on the city, causing severe damage and casualties. It was a critical blow to the Germans' transportation system in occupied France. The aim was to paralyze the French railroad system and the Allies were successful.

I was anxious to visit Pauline before classes resumed in October. She was now teaching in Bagnères-de-Bigorre, a lovely small town inland in the *Hautes* (High) Pyrénées. As soon as Maman had given her permission, I was on my bicycle pedaling with all my might toward Saint-Jean-de-

Luz. Full of hope and confidence, I presented myself at the *Kommandantur*. As I approached the front desk, a bored-looking young German soldier with hair bleached almost white by the sun looked up. Not knowing whether he spoke French, I very slowly and politely said, "*Ausweis, s'il vous plait* (Permit, please)."

He shuffled some papers on his desk, and with a blank expression picked up a paper handed it to me. I sat down to fill out the questionnaire:

Q. "Reasons for traveling?"

My runaway imagination was put to good use.

A. "Buy sheets for a hotel!"

When finished I laid the *Ausweis* application on the desk. The soldier didn't look up. I left saying, "*Merci* (Thanks)."

The form stated that it would take several days for an answer. Impatiently, I waited. When I returned to the *Kommandantur* a grumpy older soldier wearing rimless glasses was sitting behind the desk. This time I had to repeat several times what I wanted. He didn't understand me or didn't want to.

"*Ausweis, Branquet?*"

Probably I was not pronouncing the word properly. I showed him my identity card. Finally a reluctant, guttural, "*Jawohl*" crossed his thin lips. He jumped up from behind his desk, and walked into another room. It seemed that it was taking him forever. He finally returned with, surprisingly, my Ausweis in his hands. Hurrah! I suppressed my exuberance by not jumping with joy. Leaving I smiled, saying courteously, "*Merci beaucoup* (Thanks a lot)."

My thanks were totally ignored as he had gone back to his shuffling. That was all right. I had obtained what I wanted.

Happily, I took the train for Bagnères-de-Bigorre. Not being a postulant as yet Pauline was not restricted to staying in the convent. What a joy to see her on the platform waiting for me! When I got off the train, I ran toward Pauline and we fell into each other's arms. We took full advantage of the week together. We went to the movies, saw *Mary Stuart, Queen of Scots'* life. How we felt sorry for that little courageous woman who had lost her head on the block. During the whole visit we chatted, laughed, and took long walks. It was so good being reunited again. When it was time to leave, we took *vélo-taxis* (the rickshaws pulled by men on bicycles) to the railway station. To our great amusement and delight, the men decided to have a race. Pauline and I made a large bet on who was going to arrive first, one *centime* (penny). Our contagious laughter spurred them to go faster. Pedestrians stopped to watch, clapping their hands to encourage the men. During those sad times, just about anything was an occasion to break the monotony of our lives. What a treat! They arrived at the same time, no one won! I left recharged.

At the demarcation line all passengers had to get off the train in order to have their papers and bags inspected. A large wooden sign read:

"*HALT–Demarkationslinie Uberschrerten Verboten*
    (Halt–Demarcation line, no trespassing).*"

With the other passengers, I impatiently queued. Train schedules didn't mean a thing to the Germans. When my turn came, like everyone else, I opened my suitcase. The stern looking soldier with bushy eyebrows in a clipped tone asked, "*Identitat kartie* (identity card)."

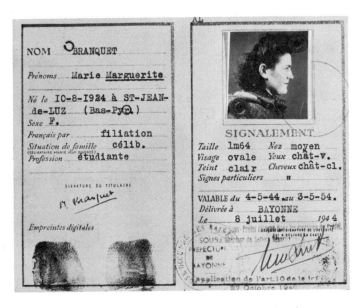

Inside of author's identity card; (below) back and front of card.

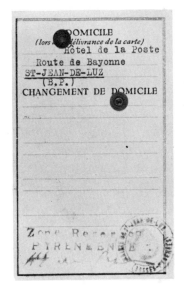

The identity card photos had to be taken in profile and fingerprints were a requirement! One could not travel without a card. After a quick look he handed it back to me. He then rummaged through my open suitcase. Among my clothes he found my Girl Scouts' book of songs. He picked it up, licking his finger. Wordlessly he slowly flipped the pages scrutinizing each one.

Oh! Yuck! I thought, German spit on my pages. Finally, he pointed to a song titled, *Le petit Japonais* (The little Japanese).

"*Was ist das* (What is it)?" With my extremely limited German I understood that much.

"*Une chanson* (A song)," I answered with a bored expression. He hastily left with the book. I could hear the other passengers grumbling impatiently behind me. He returned shortly with a short, rotund, foreboding officer with a carefully trimmed mustache.

The same stupid questions were asked, but this time in catastrophic accented French, "*Livre, quoi* (book, what)?"

The song contained the word Yokohama. It was a delightful song about a Japanese traveling on his pony to that city. Were they taking me for a young spy? It took all my willpower not to laugh in their presence. I explained that I was a kindergarten teacher. Impatiently, the officer slammed the book shut. Without another word or looking at me, he threw the book in the open suitcase and waved me through. I heard him tell the soldier, "*Mack schnell* (Hurry up)!"

Didn't they have anything better to do? When I arrived at the villa, I had a good time relating the story to my family, naturally mimicking the soldiers and their accent. Again, my clownish talent that day was put to good use.

Again and again I thought about my future. A nursing career was very appealing. After my return, while still in town, I overcame my shyness enough to visit Dr. Blazy, our family physician. I needed his advice and support to convince Maman that nursing would be a desirable career for me. He was very encouraging, mentioning that the French Red Cross had yearly free nursing courses. Watch *Le Sud-Ouest* for announcements was his recommendation. I left walking on air, first for having seen my idol alone, second for having him as an ally. My ultimate goal was to attend a nursing school in Paris and get a diploma as a surgery scrub nurse to work in a hospital. Dr. Blazy was a bachelor, tall and handsome with dark wavy hair and an irresistible smile. Before the occupation and until we left for the country, he had often been a guest at our table and a good friend of Papa's. When we moved to the apartment whenever I knew that he would visit Papa, I would make sure to be the one to open the door. How I had fallen madly in love with him! First teenage crush! No one knew. When opening the door for him I invariably blushed, and would not be able to answer his greetings.

Before the war when Papa and Michel went hunting, Dr. Blazy would often join them. Papa had always fascinated me with his hunting stories. I never tired of listening to them. My favorite: pursued by an angry wild boar, he just had time to climb a tree without dropping his rifle. He stated that he was able to kill it from the tree!! True or not I hung onto every word. One foot of the boar was preserved, and mounted on a small board, upside down. It became a peg for Papa's hunting hat. Prewar hunting seasons he would spend hours cleaning his hunting rifle, and getting all his equipment ready.

A couple days after my return, Michel had an appendicitis attack. The only way to rush him to the hospital from the villa was by horse and buggy. When he was released a problem arose. His soccer buddies decided that a buggy ride would be too bumpy for him. How to get him back from the hospital? They had a brilliant idea. On a flat cart they placed a mattress. Michel was pulled comfortably by his friends up those hills to Ohlette. How long did it take them? Who knows! Along the way, probably several bottles of wine gave them strength and comfort. That was real friendship. They were welcomed at the villa with more drinks for their efforts. Before the war Michel was the goalie of Saint-Jean-de-Luz soccer team. One year he was nominated the best non-professional goalie of France.

NOVEMBER 11, 1942
Another day of doom and treachery

November 10, in violation of the Armistice agreement, Hitler gave orders for the seizure of France's unoccupied zone. The orders were to be carried out the following day.

Hitler's letter to Field Marshal Pétain used the pretext of the Allied landing in Africa, November 8, called Operation Torch, and their possible invasion from Africa to Corsica and then France's Provence region. Hitler wanted complete control of the Mediterranean coast. He also needed the whole length of the Pyrénées Mountains to stop the smuggling of Allied airmen, Jews, escaped prisoners and young Frenchmen who didn't want to be enslaved. The Nazi regime was never successful in stopping the escapes, but many died trying with their guides.

As planned, November 11, 1942 the *Wehrmacht* invaded the unoccupied zone. Hitler had wanted the invasion to coincide with the World War I 1918 Armistice Day, the victory of France against Germany. He wanted to get even.

Le Sud-Ouest front page headlines:

Le Führer addresse un message aux Français (The *Führer* sends a message to the French).

"I had to give the order to the *Wehrmacht* to immediately go through the unoccupied zone on to areas targeted for landing by the Anglo-American troops."

The French army of one hundred thousand which remained after the 1940 armistice was unresponsive and was dissolved. The violation of the armistice by Hitler was not a total surprise. In less than twenty-four hours the *Wehrmacht's* tanks were near the French fleet port of Toulon on the Mediterranean Sea. To avert a possible escape, the *Luftwaffe* (German Air Force) blocked the port's exit with mines. French Admiral de Laborde ordered the scuttling of the mighty French fleet, preventing it from falling into the Third Reich's hands. In three weeks the Vichy government lost its empire, its small remaining army and sixty units sunk without combat; two hundred fifty thousand metric tons: two submarines, twenty-nine destroyers, seven cruisers, two battleships and one battle cruiser were sunk. Hitler didn't get the French fleet which he had so badly coveted!

ALL OF FRANCE WAS NOW OCCUPIED!
Infamy! Could it get any worse!

In December reading the paper Papa chuckled at another edict. Smiling he handed the paper to Maman, "Look
at this, Félicie."

Maman read out loud, "Within ten days all firearms,
hunting rifles, handguns must be turned in to the French
authorities. Death penalty for non-compliance."

Laughing Maman remarked, "Louis, the *Boches* don't
have a chance of finding your hunting rifles!"

The edict also mentioned that people were invited to
inform the authorities if they knew anyone who was hiding
arms. The Germans encouraged denunciations. It was
impossible for the occupation forces to check all house-
holds, and especially farms for hidden firearms, they didn't
have enough soldiers. Papa didn't have to worry about our
Basque neighbors, they also hid their hunting rifles.

The year 1942 was dragging, so much misery around
the country. By the end of December, two hundred forty
thousand French workers had left. Sauckel had reached the
goal imposed by Hitler. Was the Reich ever going to stop?
Sauckel was like an eating machine of workers. Were we
ever going to see the Germans leave our soil?

Despite the bitter weather, snow on the higher Pyrénées,
intensive escapes took place throughout the Basque Country to Spain. Without our knowledge, January 1943, Michel
had formally joined a resistance network. Due to its excellent isolated location at the foot of the mountains, our farm
was a perfect spot as a link for escape routes. From there
Michel could easily hand over the escapees to the Basque
contrebandiers or guides. His involvement is verified by the
duplicated chart from the French book, *Les Fougères de la
Liberté* (Ferns of Freedom) by Emillienne Eychenne.

ETAT NOMINATIF DES AGENTS ~~OCCASIONNELS~~ P-1

du Réseau BASE D'ESSE - Sous Réseau 4° OSSAU

NOMS ET PRENOMS DES AGENTS	DATE ET LIEU DE NAISSANCE	ADRESSE de l'Intéressé ou ses ayants cause lorsque l'Agent est décédé (1)	GRADE REEL	DATE D'ENGAGEMENT	DATE de Fin de Service	OBSERVATIONS
BRANQUET Michel	25 Janvier 1912 à OREGON (B.P.)	Hotel de la Poste JEAN DE LUZ (B.P.)		1 Janvier 1943	30-9-44	
CHIPI Jean Baptiste	1 Novembre 1909 à ONDAX (Espagne)	Maison Ukriapia ASM (B.P.)		1 Janvier 1944	30-9-44	
BAYSBAT André, Charles	3 Novembre 1898 à ORTHEZ (B.P.)	7 rue Saint Pierre THEZ (B.P.)	Chef de Bat.	1 Novembre 1943	30-9-44	
DENAS SIEU Bernde, Laurence	12 Septembre 1907 à CADALUX (Tarn)	62 rue Bayard TOULAS		1 Décembre 1942	30-9-44	
DEROUET Leonce ; Marie	30 Septembre 1889 à MASSAY (Cher)	"Les Presles" LE THEX a/LOT (Lot et Garonne)	Colonel	1 Mai 1943	30-9-44	
DRIOLLET Jean Baptiste	29 Janvier 1888 à B HORN (B.P.)	26 rue Maréchal HANNE - ST.JEAN DE LUZ (BP)		1 Janvier 1943	30-9-44	
~~DUMAHET Alexandre~~	3 Octobre 1917 à Onyox-Gare (Landes)	~~Régiment à Bue d Cordeliers 29 BAYONNE BP~~		6 Janvier 1943	30-9-44	
~~GELOS Jean Paul~~	25 Décembre 1896 USUNOME (B.P.)	Villa Nahi Naçala USUNOME (B.P.)	Cdt.	1 Novembre 1943		
~~GELOS Raymonde née Puddus~~	2 Novembre 490 NOUGUET (Gironde)	Villa Nahi Naçala USUNOME (B.P.)		1 Novembre 1943	30-9-44	
GACHAIN Martin	4 Décembre 1923 USUNOME (B.P.)	Carreul baita USUNOME (B.P.)		1 Janvier 1943	30-9-44	
GOTENAGA Jean	14 Juillet 1912 à ASCAIN (B.P.)	Maison Mirande ASCAIN (B.P.)		1 Octobre 1943	30-9-44	
GRAMONT Emile	14 Juillet 1906 à BISCAROSSE (Landes)	Villa Alexandrine des Arènes - a/POSE	Lt.d.Vais.	1 Novembre 1943	30-9-44	
HARRIE T Antoine	14 Novembre 1927 à USUNOME (B.P.)	Urohokoa à USUNOME (B.P.)		1 Janvier 1943	30-9-44	

(1) En cas de décès survenu après la Libération
(2) Pour les Etrangers, indiquer leur nationalité

Fait à PARIS , le 25 Mars 1948

LE CHEF DE RESEAU, Chef d'Escadron

Permission granted by Editions Milan, Toulouse, France.
Proof of author's brother Michel's involvement with the Résistance.

The French Résistance had an elaborate security system. Each section was isolated so the identity of the whole could not be divulged. Basques guides would not know each other. *Rendez-vous* (meeting place) between couriers were in designated public places.

Downed Allied airmen, young Frenchmen refusing to be forced to work in Germany or be drafted in the S.T.O. (French Forced Labor) and Jewish people would arrive by train in Saint-Jean-de-Luz, usually from Paris. They were met outside the station then directed to the nearby *Café Cosmopolitain.* All sorts of disguises were used, workers clothes, even one daring man dressed as a French police- man. From there a *passeur* (courier) escorted them to a safe house, and without our knowledge some to our farm. Papa was the only member of the family who helped Michel. The Basque *contrebandiers* or guides would set out on foot with the escapees after dark, through the *Col d'Ibardin* (mountain pass of Ibardin) to Spain and freedom.

Upon their arrival in Spain escapees were escorted to a camp. The route to England would take them from San Sebastian in the Basque part of Spain to Madrid, Gibraltar and finally London.

The *Abwehr* (German Army Intelligence) was never able to break that network. Some other networks were not as successful. Under the Geneva Convention, soldiers who were caught could claim prisoner-of-war status. The Gestapo treated the civilian people who helped them brutally and more often than not it meant certain death after horrible torture. The *Abwehr* staged many "human" hunts.

Thanks to the dedication of their countrymen, approximately two hundred thousand out of three hundred thousand French Jews survived. Archbishop Saliège of Toulouse located many Catholic homes or convents where Jewish children were hidden for the duration of the occupation. When I was young I didn't know what a Jewish person was, everyone was French.

French saboteurs were the most successful of all the occupied countries. It was partly due to France's location on the map of Europe, its excellent railroad and canal system. The *Résistance*, with the help of Allied airdrops of arms, were able to accomplish great feats of sabotage. The airdrops were coordinated by messages heard on the BBC French language broadcasts. They were meaningless to the Germans. Into the Peugeot factory, now a tank factory, explosives were smuggled and installed, then exploded near the most valuable machinery where intensive damage was reported.

Général de Gaulle from his London Headquarters estab-
lished the *FFI, Forces Françaises de l'Intérieur* (Interior
French Forces) who could coordinate their efforts with the
Résistance.

February 1943, a grim month! The Germans took
complete control of supplies. After taking their lion's share
followed by the middlemen of the black market and the
farmers, very little reached the consumers!

AGAIN! *VERBOTEN*—interdiction of queuing in front
of stores!

What a ridiculous order! No alternative was proposed.
Was the Third Reich afraid of spoiling their image? Strangely,
there was no punishment for disobeying this order.

Dreadful orders with grave consequences were issued by
the puppet Vichy regime. Laval decreed the formation of a
new police, *La Milice* (militia). It would be under the
direction of the hated Waffen SS Joseph Darnaud. It set
off instinctive waves of hostility from the French people.
Vichy courts offered felons the choice of joining the Milice
or prison. To the disgust and dismay of the majority of our
nation it became a French Gestapo, a political police. Their
mission was to maintain order against the French Communists, Jews, the underground, the Gaullists or anti-
Vichy. The Milice was manipulated by the Germans and
actively cooperated with the dreaded SS and Gestapo. The
Germans found them most efficient especially against
members of the Résistance. They became the scourge of
the Résistance.

The Milice became a tool of terror made up of thugs
and cutthroats. Their viciousness and cruelty toward their
countrymen at times surpassed the Gestapo's. The organ-

izing of the Milice was the start of a hidden civil war—
French against French, La Milice handing their countrymen to the enemy.

The Vichy government was sinking into inhumanity,
ordering the dissolution of all charitable organizations
including the Salvation Army. Since 1940 these associa-
tions had helped by feeding and clothing so many French
people. My parents were appalled, especially Maman who
was always involved in community service.

Nazi controlled Vichy-France had stamps printed with
Pétain's photograph. République Française (French Republic) no longer appeared on them, only Postes Françaises
(French Postal Service). Never before had a living person
appeared on French stamps, but Pétain, yes!

More protests in March against STO (Forced French
Labor), especially that all males twenty-three to thirty-one
had to register at Hôtels de Villes (Town Halls).

We could not understand that despite the fact that all
of France was now occupied, the demarcation line was still
in effect.

Finally early March brought one good surprise! The
German Authorities declared that an Ausweis would no
longer be necessary to cross the demarcation line. We could
hardly believe it! Now I would be able to travel to visit
Pauline without the Germans' permission. Strict control of
identity cards remained mandatory.

The German soldiers methodically continued to inspect
suitcases, wallets and purses. The journey to visit Pauline
was still quite an adventurous undertaking.

Traveling by train was greatly facilitated despite the
rundown wagons and erratic schedules. One never knew

when a train was going to leave or arrive on time because of the German troops' priority.

Families separated for three long years were now able to visit each other again. Even though censorship was not lifted, interzonal postcards were discarded. Slowly postal service resumed, practically back to normal between the two zones. I started writing weekly letters to Pauline giving her details of our daily country life. The good news about the demarcation line was severely dampened by the severe increase of meat rationing. To eat, clothe, and heat oneself became a constant obsession of the average Frenchman, especially in the large cities. Patience not being a natural trait of the French, those constant problems tested their nerves to the fullest. Parisians suffered badly under the shortages, struggling desperately for existence.

The daily requirement is 2400 calories for most people; only half was allocated to workers. The rest of the population obtained what they could. Many stores closed their doors due to lack of supplies.

More restrictions! Food packages for French prisoners of war and drafted workers mailed with great sacrifices by their families were reduced from fifty to twenty kilograms. They already were on a starvation diet.

VERBOTEN VERBOTEN VERBOTEN VERBOTEN

Not a month passed without something added to the list of FORBIDDEN things to do. Because of their independent natures, the French resented all those restrictions, and especially the petty ones. As times got tougher, the French ingenuity increased.

Another decree, *VERBOTEN* to sell T.S.F (radios)

The Germans were probably more and more exasperated with the directives, encouragement, and veiled messages received from de Gaulle on the French speaking BBC broadcasts from London. They had reason to be! It was estimated that most of the owners of radios in France listened to the BBC. The broadcasts still started with the welcome:

Ici, Londres (Here, London).

After the American landing in Sicily, July 10, 1943, called "Operation Husky," French people were hopeful for an imminent landing in France.

The greatly reduced German occupation forces didn't know how to cope with the French conniving mind, called the *system D*, the D for *débrouillard* (resourceful). In our area they were still baffled by the Basques, their mysterious language and culture. Basques were known for not being afraid of taking risks. The Gestapo was flustered by their daredevil ways of smuggling people into Spain.

From the beginning of the occupation the Pyrénées Mountains had been a major problem to the Germans. Soldiers patrolled heavily National 10, the railway from Paris to the border at Hendaye, some secondary Basque roads and part of the mountains. The mountains remained a sieve. Over the past three years, the Germans were painfully aware of that phenomenon, the *contrebandiers*, who had the advantage of knowing the terrain. Only the *contrebandiers* had the confidence to make good use of the frequent dense fog and tall ferns. These advantages gave them stronger security against German discovery.

A unique signal used by the Basques in the mountains is the *irrintzina*, a bizarre laugh/scream sounding like repeating Aie, Aie up to a very high pitched scream and down the scale ending with a sort of a laugh. It was often used as coded language. If no one had ever heard it before in the middle of the night, it could be blood curdling. The Germans didn't like dealing with the Basques on account of their extremely ferociously independent natures, and their dislike of rules.

In the Basque region, the Germans demanded a census of sheep and donkeys. Grazing in the Pyrénées Mountains was forbidden within three kilometers of the Spanish border. They were afraid of the many opportunities for escapes. People were being smuggled as sheepherders among the flocks of sheep, others rode donkeys through the mountains passes. The order was disastrous for the Basque farmers. *Tonton* Joseph's flock of sheep needed to feed during the summer months in the high mountains. He also needed to cut the furze growing on the mountains which he used as fodder for his cattle.

My cousin Paco related a crisis they had in the mountains after the census request.

"At four in the morning, *Attata* (Dad in Basque) and I went to the mountain summer fields where our sheep were feeding. We needed to bring them down for shearing. German soldiers in pairs were patrolling the Pyrénées Mountains. They were equipped with shotguns, binoculars and German Shepherd dogs. The soldiers were trigger happy, always looking for people escaping to Spain, but scared of the Basque *contrebandiers* who had no qualms in killing them. All of sudden bullets started to whistle around us.

Scared, we threw ourselves on the ground. When we dared looked up the soldiers signaled us to come down toward them. We had no choice but to do so. They inspected our *Ausweis* which were in order. At the sound of the bullets, the sheep had panicked and scattered. *Attata* and I had to start all over again. Due to the rising temperature it became harder for us to gather the flock. It is easier to get them together when it is cooler. We had left at four in the morning, we didn't return to the farm until two in the afternoon. We were shaken up and exhausted. *Ama* (Mom in Basque) had been so worried when she had not seen us return earlier."

It seemed that in times of trouble, problems multiplied. As on a lot of French farms, in the spring our potato fields were invaded by the Colorado Beetle. It became a back-breaking job, up and down the rows with a jar collecting those ugly bugs by hand. They would hide under the leaves. It had to be done! Either them or no potatoes. How tired we all became of that chore!

The hard farm work, due to my age, didn't affect me like the rest of the family. On the contrary it made me very strong physically. Michel, in his early thirties, was robust like most Basques. In 1943 Papa and Maman were respectively sixty-two and fifty-eight. They had lived for twenty years in comfort, working hard to build a successful hotel business. It must have been very difficult for them to adjust.

Vichy-France was collaborating more and more with the Nazis. Waffen SS Joseph Darnaud declared it his absolute priority to catch young people who didn't want to work in

German factories. In protest, a resurgence of acts of sabotage, especially of railways hit the country. Rails were unriveted thus not cutting the power connected to the signals, derailing trains going over loose tracks.

For the first time the Résistance killed a member a the dreaded *Milice*. It was followed by severe reprisals on hostages and summary executions. The Milice was not enough, a decree was posted that Frenchmen could now sign up and join the dreaded Waffen SS. It was France's greatest disgrace.

Summer 1943 saw a resurgence of sabotage of bridges and the vital extensive French canal system. At one time three thousand barges were stranded. It was the result of a well planned act of sabotage by *one* Frenchman! It took the Germans four months to complete the repairs which were blown up again by the same man. What a *tour de force* (Feat of strength)!

During his regular visits to town Papa saw Ignacio, still in the employ of the Germans, in the street. He told him that the Germans soldiers on R & R had very low morale, five had committed suicide. One soldier was seen crying, an officer asked the reason,

"I just received a letter. My whole family died in a bombing."

The officer slapped him, "It is not important! Only the *Führer* and the Reich count!" The soldier, infuriated, lunged at him and was shot on the spot. He was buried without a service in the local cemetery. Flowers were seen on his unmarked grave deposited by unknown persons.

When Papa returned from his trips to town he always brought back the latest issues of *Le Sud-Ouest* for Michel

and the Catholic newspaper *La Croix* (The Cross) for
Maman. I was finally allowed to read the paper, a sign that
at practically nineteen I was accepted in the adult world.
Naturally without my parents knowledge I had been reading the paper whenever I could. Scanning through one of
the back issues I noticed a small article. *La Croix-Rouge
Française* (French Red Cross) of Saint-Jean-de-Luz was
organizing a year-long course for women who wanted to be
Aide Médico-Sociale (Practical nurse and medical social
aide). The classes would begin in October, and would last
the school year 1943-44. The love of my life, Dr. Blazy, had
been right! I could not contain my excitement. Finally,
an opportunity to attend the classes I had eagerly been
looking forward to taking. A ray of hope for my future.
The only last obstacle was to get Maman's approval, no
sense asking Papa. In the past, whenever we had approached him with a request his invariable answer had
been, "Ask your mother."

I found her in the kitchen where she spent a lot of time.
I took a deep breathe going right to the point, "Maman, I
would like to attend the Red Cross nurse's training." Her
instant answer was—"YES, you can." I could not believe
my ears! I was ecstatic, finally I had a future ahead of me.
Plans were taking shape, after graduation I would enroll in
a Catholic nursing school in Paris for two more years and
get my nurse's degree. I am sure that without Dr. Blazy's
support I would not have received her consent. Strict
Maman had changed so much, as we all did, that it was
hard to predict her answers.

Before I started my classes Maman and I went to visit
Pauline in Nevers, the seat of her religious order's Mother

House. The town was about 600 kilometers north. Pauline was starting her novitiate which would last six months. We were again so happy to see each other, but now she was no longer free to leave the Mother House. It dampened the visit as I felt a wall was separating us. I was losing her some more. Soon she would no longer be my sister Pauline, but *Soeur Marie-Ange* (Sister Mary Angel).

On the way back the train had to make an unscheduled stop, the Orléans bridge had been bombed and destroyed by the Allies during our stay in Nevers. Everyone had to get off. Valises in hand, Maman and I joined the other passengers walking in difficult terrain in order to reach the train waiting for us on the other side of the damaged bridge. It was no easy task as no one had appropriate shoes to tackle that descent followed by climbing out of the ravine. It was much easier for me than poor Maman who was fifty-nine, and had lost a lot of weight. She was not used to walking. Being young, for me it was another adventure.

Upon my return I started my Red Cross courses. A white nurse's uniform, including a white veil, had to be obtained. Due to clothing rations, it was not an easy task. Sheets from the hotel hidden from the Germans were used. Several fittings later with the help of our deft, long time seamstress, I was proudly wearing my new uniform with a red cross on the veil. Attending the courses meant daily commuting by bicycle from the villa, quite a performance on those country roads and in all kinds of weather. During the winter Maman stuffed newspapers under my sweater as the wind could be very sharp, especially coasting down-hill from the mountains. I had outgrown my coat and we were unable to buy another one. Being the tallest of the family, I could not get a hand-me-down. That sweater had been quite an undertaking as my first attempt at knitting. It was made from another unraveled sweater whose wool had been dyed dark blue. I was so proud of my chef-d'oeuvre (masterpiece), even more because my siblings had said that I would never finish it.

The course was very interesting. That kind of a career fitted well with my personality of caring for others. Finally I had found my niche. Maman had instilled in me the importance of helping others, another one of her legacies. Most of our practical training was done at the free dispensary run by the Sisters of Charity. We practiced giving injections using rubber balls. I'll never forget the first time I had to give one to a human. It helped that it was injected him in the fesses (backside). I was positioned behind the man needle in hand when he asked, "Are you experienced?" Trembling behind his back, I answered, "Mais oui, Monsieur! I give injections all the time."

At the dispensary, when the nun in charge was not available, we had to make our own diagnosis and treat the patients the best we could. Most of them came to the dispensary for minor problems. We sometimes were sent to treat people in the countryside. Usually it was an assignment the student nurses fought over because the farmers always thanked us with eggs, cheese or vegetables.

One of my cases was to a care for a woman, Madame Ibarrart, at a farm located on the way to the villa. When I arrived at her door I was greeted by an elderly, tiny, but plump, and aproned woman dressed in black. Her hair was tightly and severely pulled back in a chignon wrapped as the Basque custom in a snood of the same color. After the death of a family member, Basque women wear black for one year signifying that they are in mourning, then grey for a year or two. As the families are usually very large, Basque women end up wearing black for most of their lives. I never saw Maman in lively colors, mostly grey or sometimes mauve or lavender.

"*Egun on* (Good morning in Basque)," *Madame* Ibarrart said ushering me in, her softly wrinkled face breaking into a smile.

Several weeks later the treatment was finished. To thank me for my visits, *Madame* Ibarrart offered me a glass of her homemade liqueur. It would have been bad manners to refuse. The first sip practically burned my insides. She insisted that I finish. I thought that I could not endure the torture! Finally I was able to politely leave, *Madame* Ibarrart following me with her multitude of "*Milesker ainitz* (Thank you very much in Basque)."

I left saying a few Basque words I knew, "*Ikus arte* (Goodbye)."

When I got on my bicycle the road was weaving. As soon as I arrived at the villa, Maman looked at me quizzically, "Whatever is the matter with you? Are you sick?" she asked.

I could only mumble, "I think I am drunk!"

It was a miracle that I had not fallen off my bicycle. Maman had to help me up the stairs. After a good nap I was fit again. We all had a good laugh at my first drunkenness. No reprimand, Maman understood Basque customs.

When I went to Saint-Jean-de-Luz to attend my nursing classes, my brother Michel would sometimes ask me to deliver messages to some of his friends. Most of them were to his soccer team buddies. I became his telephone wire. The messages were all verbal and often didn't make sense. I would have to repeat them, his instructions were very strict, "Listen carefully. You must repeat them exactly as I told you."

Impatiently I would answer, "*D'accord. D'accord* (Okay. Okay)!"

I didn't understand what all the fuss was about. They were only dumb messages which didn't make sense! I recall pedaling out of my way to deliver one message to Michel's friend Pierre. That particular, seemingly garbled, message was: "*En fin de semaine les poissons seront achetés au prix courant* (At the end of the week fish will be purchased at current price)." Pierre, an hotel owner was my friend Odile's, who lived in Ascain, brother-in-law. He had been arrested years earlier by the Germans and promptly released. Without my knowledge Michel was using me as a runner to deliver messages for the Résistance.

One day after noticing that our chickens were constantly scratching themselves Michel went to town to get the vet. He found that they were covered with minuscule vermin. Injections were prescribed, but who was going to do it? Being a nurse in training, I was elected for that unsavory task! After all I knew how to give injections to humans! Doing it to chickens should be an easy task. One evening before going to bed, I locked the chicken coop. The following day, bright and very early I bravely entered, quickly closing the door after me. The rooster and chickens scattered noisily, feathers flying all around me. Perhaps they wondered, what was this big animal without feathers doing in their adobe? It was quite a chore catching them one at a time, injecting and releasing them outside. After a lot of chasing, cackling, feather losses and exhaustion, especially on my part, I let out a sigh of relief. A messy chore accomplished.

As I was walking back to the villa, it didn't take long for me feel itchy and, like the chickens, I started scratching. The mites were taking their revenge, looking for and finding a larger victim. Very unhappy to have been dislodged from a very lucrative steady diet! The vet had not mentioned that these mites liked humans only for a short while, just long enough to drive them crazy. My clothes had to be boiled to kill them. A long warm bath helped the itching. Papa and Maman didn't really show it but I felt that they were grateful for a job well done.

Food had become so scarce that Rumania sent 700 metric tons of food to the French National Relief. Soup kitchens remained available to help some of the starving Parisians. At the farm our years of hard work had kept us well fed. When I left for my daily classes I never left empty handed. Supplies were loaded on my bicycle for my sister Marie and family, my pal Léon, his parents and many other needy people.

Maman had some special elderly lonely people that she asked me to visit. "When you make your deliveries," she would admonish, "talk to them, stay a while." She was teaching me to how to "care" for others especially the elderly.

In town electricity was rationed, it naturally didn't effect us. As bad as the carbide lamps were, they served us well. It was early to bed and up with daylight. In our little corner of the world we were more than isolated, but due to my parents' insight we were safe, and had enough to eat. Stylish clothes were not important in the country.

Late August, Sauckel wanted an additional five hundred thousand French workers! Panic hit all eligible Frenchmen. More and more young men joined the underground, others made their way south to escape into Spain. Women of Paris again demonstrated against the departures of workers for Germany.

By October all men age eighteen to fifty were required to always have in their possession a worker's certificate. Without them, precious ration cards would not be issued. As far as the Germans were concerned my brother Michel didn't exist, Papa was too old. But three first cousins fell in that category. Even though farmers were exempt, our cousin Pierre had been drafted with the excuse that he was not needed. Léon's address was changed to our farm.

In November, Von Ribbentrop, Third Reich Minister of Foreign Affairs wrote that, "...the only way and unique way to maintain calm and public order within France is with the *Wehrmacht*."

Cousin Olga's letters continued to keep us abreast of the capital news better than our local newspaper. She always had some interesting happenings. She wrote that often German soldiers were seen in Paris streets with their easels, painting the capital scenes! What a contrast from the harshness of the occupation for the French.

New Year! 1944

Night has fallen over Europe.

Another year of my youth stolen. We were all despairing. How long would the detested German occupation last?

Eighteen years after writing *Mein Kampf*, Adolf Hitler was dreaming of his "Big Reich" engulfing the world. He envisioned his colonial empire lasting for more than a thousand years with the help of his demonic dream of enslaving nations.

The fourth year under German occupation started with a rise in acts of sabotage. Many factories were dynamited by the Résistance.

Early 1944 word filtered down that General Rommel stayed at the *Hôtel de la Poste*. He was in town inspecting the Basque coast *Atlantikwall*. It was again declared impassable! BBC broadcasts started to give hints of a possible invasion. The Nazis wondered how or where the Allies might attack.

March 27, was a bright, sunny, crisp day with a hint of spring in the air. We were just finishing a late lunch. Strange muffled noises, "boom, boom, boom" were heard from far away. It was at regular intervals. We looked at each other with puzzled looks. None of us could identify this unusual sound.

I quickly said, "I'll run to the attic and climb on the roof. Maybe I'll be able to see something."

The roof was easily accessible through the third floor attic bedrooms, but I was the only one agile enough to perform that gymnastic. Due to the excellent visibility I could see bellowing dark smoke in the far distance, but not from the direction of Saint-Jean-de-Luz, it was much farther north. By the time I had reached the roof the whole family had hurriedly gone out leaving their unfinished lunch on the table. I saw them standing in the front yard looking up, shielding their eyes with their hands against the sun. They were anxiously waiting for details of what I was seeing. I screamed down, "Lots of dark smoke far away."

We were all puzzled, we had never heard similar noise. What could it be? The family would have to wait for answers until the following day when I returned from my classes.

The next day, as soon as I arrived in town I rushed to the tobacco shop to buy *Le Sud-Ouest*. The owner, *Monsieur* Irigoyen told me what had happened while I was scanning the "shocking" headlines. "*C'est pas possible* (It's not possible)!" I told him.

"Read on" he said, "all the details are in the paper."

PARME AIRPORT BOMBED
BY THE AMERICAN AIR FORCE

"In two waves the 8th American Air Force planes at noon crossed French Brittany flying toward Biarritz where they dropped their first bomb at 2:25 pm."

On the twentieth the BBC had broadcast a strange message:

Les violettes de Parme vont fleurir (Violets of Parme are going to bloom). It was a coded message warning a select few of the bombing of Biarritz!

The Basque region after nearly four years of occupation had been peaceful except the small incident of 1942 when the British ship fired at the Germans' fortifications. Very little damage, no deaths. This time it was quite different. West of the airport was located the town of Biarritz, my brother-in-law Paul's hometown. The main targets were the railway station and the Parme airport a couple of miles away. The station was a difficult target in the middle of town. The damage had been done on a straight line hitting private homes. The railway station was completely destroyed, more than 100 civilians dead, and many buildings were reported destroyed. Two American bombers were downed by German anti-aircraft guns.

The main target, the paper stated, had been the Bréget factory near the airport which was building German transport planes, Voss 144, and the observation planes, Foche-Wulf 189. The airfield had also been used to train *Luftwaffe* pilots on the Arado 96 and Messerschmitt 109. Great damage was done to the factory. German planes were pulverized on the airport tarmac. Surrounding airports of Bordeaux, Pau and two others were also bombed. Parme airfield was completely destroyed and would remain unusable.

Biarritz is located twenty kilometers north of Saint-Jean-de-Luz, on the Atlantic coast. It is a beautiful summer resort with a well renowned reputation in western Europe. In the mid-eighteen hundreds the town had been discovered and made famous by Princess Eugénie, wife of Napoléon III. It became their summer capital and was also the favorite residence of Edward VII of England and King Alphonse XIII of Spain. Both were frequent visitors.

My brother-in-law Paul's mother barely escaped death when the building adjacent to her house collapsed. Like most *Biarrots* (inhabitants of the city), she had gone to her second floor window to investigate the unusual noise. Buildings were collapsing around her. She ran downstairs screaming looking for her husband. They were miraculously spared. The daylight bombing had been totally unexpected by the Germans, and even more so by the local people. No sirens had sounded.

Wonderful rumors started to float—possible invasion by the Allies, but where? Could it be Saint-Jean-de-Luz with its natural, well-sheltered, deep and large bay? It was good news, but still scary because if it was going to be on the Basque coast we surely would be bombed. These were tense weeks. We had also been afraid of bombings because the Germans had started to build a wooden pier for submarine refueling. One day the weather had been in our favor! The pier, during a severe storm, was totally destroyed by pounding waves.

Due to my daily trips to town I kept the family abreast of the latest news. My older sister Marie's husband Paul faithfully listened to the forbidden BBC French broadcasts. I became the purveyor of news gathered also at the dispensary. The other student nurses would tell me what their fathers had heard. How we discussed the life we would have after the Germans' departure. How nice it would be to be a free teenager, to be able to see Paris for the first time, start going to the movies, dance without having those *sales Boches* (dirty Krauts) around.

The BBC news was getting more and more encouraging. Invasion was a new word often heard during the programs. Newspapers controlled by the Germans emphasized that it would be suicidal for the Allies to try a landing. One only had to see the imposing 2000 mile *Atlantikwall* fortifications! The German High Command kept on insisting that NO ONE could possibly go through!

Late May my classes were completed. I was looking forward to receiving my French Red-Cross certificate of completion: *Aide Médico-Sociale*

Author wearing the official French Red Cross uniform

Author accomplished her first major goal, earning her French Red Cross diploma.

One year of difficult commuting by bicycle, in all kinds of weather had not been in vain. I had accomplished the first major goal of my life. Now I could look forward to someday attending the nursing school in Paris. After graduation we were committed to do volunteer work for the French Red Cross as our classes had been free. I continued going to the dispensary, a nursery and working as a nurse-intern at a hospital in Bayonne.

During that school year I went swimming as often as possible with a few friends. Maman was opposed to it as she strongly believed in abnegation. Sacrifice would be like a prayer to end the war. It was too much to ask of a teenager, I was not about to give up my only form of recreation. It entailed fibbing to Maman which, unfortunately, I became very good at.

After graduation, Maman agreed to let me visit Pauline who was now teaching at a convent school in Tulle, a town located in central France. Even by train it was not easily accessible. In January a train traveling in the direction of Tulle had been sabotaged and derailed, leaving twenty-five dead. Fortunately, my parents didn't hear about it until I returned from my journey.

That trip was quite unforgettable. At dawn one day in the early part of the last week of May, I left the villa on my bicycle, my backpack well secured. I was also carrying fruit and fresh vegetables for Pauline. Maman had prepared sandwiches for the journey. At the railway station I left the bicycle at the checkroom. I changed trains in Bordeaux for the second leg of the trip. It was a secondary line so we stopped at all the small stations and didn't travel at great speed. The wagons were old and rickety. The Germans had taken the best train cars to carry their troops. Consequently the wagons were always very crowded. It was horrendous, hardly any space to move, many people were sitting in the aisles on their suitcases, some flopped on the floor. I rode most of the trip on the steps, at least I had fresh air. At our slow speed it was not risky, the only danger was the possibility of the rails being dynamited by the Résistance. Was I minimizing the danger? Young people of different eras have confidence that they are immortal. As usual, an exciting trip. Everything was an adventure!

When I arrived in Tulle, I was surprised not to see Pauline at the railway station. It concerned me. I took a *vélo-taxi* to the convent. Tulle seemed such a far away town from the mainstream of France, very backward compared to the resort town of Saint-Jean-de-Luz. At the convent I was advised that *Soeur Marie-Ange* was still in class. It was such a pleasure seeing each other again. I brought her up to date on all the family news. The following days, during the classes, I visited the peaceful town, made a few purchases. The meals were taken with the nuns at which time we didn't get the opportunity to talk. A penance for me! We caught up during the week-end when we walked in the countryside. After a week and half it was time to go home. We said our sad goodbyes, we never knew when our next visit would be. As at the villa we naturally didn't have a telephone it had been decided that I would return June 5.

As soon as the train left Tulle we were caught in a bad storm with torrential rain and strong winds. My compartment was naturally overcrowded, and water started to leak through the roof, there was no room for me to move any place else. By the time I got off the train in Bordeaux for my transfer I was soaked through and through.

When I arrived in Saint-Jean-de-Luz I picked up my
bicycle at the station and pedaled with all my might to the
villa. As soon as I arrived Maman gave me a hot toddy.
How welcome would a hot bath be! After removing my
clothes, shock! My torso had turned blue...not from the
cold but from the sweater dye! The scrubbing didn't help
much, I was quite a sight! I felt so bad about losing the
now shrunken sweater that I had so lovingly knitted. I had
to throw away my first knitting masterpiece. There was
enough time to get a good rest and the following day I
needed to return to the dispensary.

**It is not enough to know the past, it is necessary to
understand it.**

–Paul Claudel

Chapter 9

Posterity! You shall never know how much it costs the present generation to preserve your freedom. I hope, you will make good use of it.

–John Adams, U.S. President, 1797

June 6, 1944, I was at the dispensary with two other nurses when Sister Catherine came flying in all excited, her habit in disarray, her Rosary clicking at her side. We immediately stopped what we were doing because Sister had always been so reserved.

"*Les Américains ont débarqué* (The Americans have landed)!"

She excitedly exclaimed. How could one express surprise after waiting four long years to be liberated?

Astounded, in unison we cried out, "*Quoi* (What)?"

Nurse Mireille, always a defeatist, turned around looking at all of us, "*C'est un canard* (It's a hoax)."

"No, no," replied Sister Catherine, "I heard it on the BBC news."

Forgetting our patients, we started talking all at once, laughing, hugging each other. I could not wait until I conveyed the wonderful news to the family.

D-DAY

A date that shook the world. A date in which history took a turn that gave Western Europe hope. It left us all breathless!

The welcome American invasion in Normandy!

It rang the death throes of the Third Reich.

Doomed Hitler's monstrous, evil Nazi Germany.

June 5, Hitler didn't know that his steely grip was going to be pried open, starting to clear a continent of his tyranny. The invasion had been the best kept secret ever. We didn't think of an Allied landing. *It was American!* The invasion could never have happened without the American war production and collective achievements of millions of Americans from factory workers to farmers who grew the food for the troops.

It was the biggest Crusade, delivering Europe from Hitler's tyranny and barbaric tentacles. It was going to shake the foundation of Nazi Germany. In our quiet little corner of the world, so far away from Normandy, we had no idea of what a landing entailed.

The Germans had been taken completely by surprise at the audacity of the landing. In France the *Atlantikwall* was the most fortified. But, after all, the Americans launched three successful previous landings November 8, 1942 in Africa, and two in Italy—Sicily, July 10, 1943 and Salerno September 9, 1943.

"*Zie Kommen* (They are arriving)."

were the only words that came out of the Atlantikwall Germans sentries at the costal defenses of Normandy. A wall that had been declared impregnable. Even the officers could not believe that the landing had started.

The German high command had always stubbornly believed that an invasion might be attempted at the closest land between England and France, *Pas-de-Calais* (Strait of Dover) only twenty miles across. Bad weather had also given the German High Command a false sense of safety. The Americans could not possibly attempt a landing in that kind of weather! It was predicted to get worse. Hitler, blinded by his own importance and power had thought that discipline and complete faith in HIM would win over democracy.

By a quirk of fate, General Rommel had left Normandy for Germany on June 4 to celebrate his wife's birthday which fell on June 6. Before his departure he had been given the latest weather reports. BAD! Hitler was sleeping late! His entourage didn't want to wake him up. Had General Rommel not left, might it have changed the outcome of the invasion? He would have been able to be near Normandy and closer to the action.

During the night American paratroopers had touched ground in the little town of *Sainte-Mère-l'Eglise*. Its inhabitants were the first French to be liberated. The paratroopers were protected by eleven thousand planes.

At dawn, on June 6, five thousand vessels, fifty thousand men, fifteen hundred tanks, three thousand assorted military vehicles were in a hundred miles of open water on their way to Normandy. Waves and waves of young soldiers, many sea sick, landed from Higgins landing crafts (called after the designer, Andrew Jackson Higgins) hurling themselves on the beach, struggling in cold water waist deep, fighting their way ashore on the sands of Omaha Beach. It was not easy as the weather had not cooperated and the landing crafts were fighting choppy waters. The invasion was twenty miles wide!

Men from different countries besides America participated in the landing; British, Canadians, Free French and Polish all fought to free Europe from slavery. They had come into the darkness. It was the greatest orchestrated invasion in the world's recorded history. Ships of all sizes synchronized to the minute. It was the biggest Armada ever seen.

Code-name, "Operation Overlord"

It was the start of disaster after disaster for Nazi Germany which would within a year be destroyed.

On June 1, the BBC had broadcast the first two verses of last century French poet Verlaine's *Chanson d'Automne* (Fall song). It was a pre-arranged signal to the FFI (Free French Forces) and the Résistance to sabotage and lend their support in preparation for the imminent landing.

"*Les sanglots longs* (The long sobs)
Des violons (Of the violins)"

In 1942 the *Atlantikwall* blueprints had been stolen by a Frenchman, then smuggled to England. By radio contacts with the Allies, the Résistance had continuously sent valuable information on the wall's weak spots as it had been built mostly by Frenchmen. The coded messages also passed information on the tides, beach obstacles, number of German units and troop movements. Those messages greatly helped the success of the landing. Résistance members' courage and knowledge of the countryside were of invaluable help, cutting combat short by weeks. Its members constantly harassed the retreating *Wehrmacht*, blowing up more trains than the Allied air strikes. They had set in motion severe sabotage; six hundred trains were derailed, telephone wires cut. On their own the French underground liberated many towns. The FFI (French Free Troops) captured forty-two thousand Germans.

"German soldiers were throwing away their weapons and giving up...there weren't enough soldiers to guard them...they marched in long lines without weapons under the command of their own officers...how young they were...in their early teens with uniforms too large for their young bodies..."[3]

Fierce fighting was reported around the hedgerows some as tall as five feet, which separate farmland plots, making excellent concealment for the Germans. By 1944 many Germans soldiers were very young, or older, because since 1943 the Reich had been fighting on three fronts.

From Vichy, Nazi controlled Field Marshal Pétain broadcast his revolting message to stand by the Germans who had strict orders to shoot on the spot anyone suspected of cooperating with the Allied Forces.

On that glorious day, June 6, before I left Saint-Jean-de-Luz, I stopped by Marie's. As soon as she opened the door we started to talk excitedly. We still could not believe it. After FOUR YEARS it had finally happened. As neither Marie nor her husband Paul had bicycles I was really the only one mobile at a moment's notice. I left in a hurry to bring the exciting news to the rest of the family at the villa.

---

3   Charles P. Arnot, retired ABC News correspondent, thirty-five years as a foreign correspondent, including WWII service in the European and Pacific theaters, and author of *Don't Kill the Messenger*

How we had prayed for that miraculous day!

Never had I been so happy in four years. I pedaled with wings, whistling all the way up to the villa, rehearsing in my head how I would announce the news. No sooner was I at the gate than I threw my bicycle on the ground screaming the loudest I had ever done,

"The Americans have landed in Normandy," time and time again then ran, ran, ran to the front door. By that time Papa and Maman were at the front steps.

Papa turned toward Maman, repeating, "It is not possible, Félicie."

Maman didn't say a word. I saw silent tears rolling down her cheeks.

Papa added, "Quick, Maita, go to the farm and fetch Michel."

When we came back Papa had a bottle of champagne open. After a couple of glasses he decided, "We have to go to *Tonton* Joseph's and bring him the good news. I will take several bottles of champagne with us."

The four of us happily walked the two kilometers. It was one time Maman didn't object to my whistling. When we arrived a short distance from the farm, I started to run, my feet hardly touched the ground. I wanted to be the first one to spread the good news. What a reunion! My cousin Pasco was dispatched to tell the closest neighbors. I naturally went with him. The news would be disseminated from farm to farm, even to the most remote ones.

I was heady thinking of the Germans' departure. The following day when I saw them in town I smirked inside. You don't know it as yet, but you are defeated and you are leaving soon! You are *KAPUT* (done for)!

But, it was just as well that we didn't realize that it would take more than two months to see the last of the Germans. I had hoped that we would be liberated before my twentieth birthday, August 10, but it was not to be. To live again! To come and go as we pleased, walk on our beach, swim where we wanted. Never to listen to that detested language. My teenage years were now OVER, stolen, never to be replaced, but not my youth and spirit!

After the allied landing, in desperation the Gestapo had redoubled their efforts to catch anyone in Saint-Jean-de-Luz or Ciboure helping anyone cross the Pyrénées to Spain.

June 8, smiling I walked into the dispensary still in my euphoric state shouting a resounding, "*Bonjour*, everyone." I was greeted by heavy silence. "What's going on?" I asked. "Have you already forgotten that we are going to be liberated soon?"

Sister Catherine, I saw had been crying, "This morning the Gestapo arrested more than thirty *Luziens*, all part of an underground smuggling network, including its chief. We were told that they had been betrayed to the dreaded Gestapo by a *Luzien*. How can anyone do such an horrible thing to people living in the same town?"

"Who was arrested?" My heart felt squeezed by anxiety. I might know some of them.

Haltingly Sister Catherine answered, "*Monsieur* Laffargue from the leather good store on *rue Gambetta*."

"Oh! No," I exclaimed. I had often made purchases with Maman at his store.

Sister Catherine looking at me, hesitated, "Also someone you know very well," she paused with a heavy sigh, "Dr. Blazy."

"It's not possible!" I cried out, "not him!"

For the first time in my life I learned the feeling of hate, first hate for the person, a *Luzien* who had betrayed Dr. Blazy to the Gestapo. How would I be able to convey the horrible news to the family? That evening when I arrived at the villa I found Papa relaxing in an easy chair. How could I tell him? I knelt next to his chair, looked up and hesitantly said, "Papa, the Gestapo have arrested Dr. Blazy."

He jumped out of his chair, looking down at me he barely whispered, "Phillip?"

I could only nod. Stiffly, without a word, Papa walked away. Later our dinner was eaten in total silence. Papa didn't mention Dr. Blazy's name again. From that day on, he was a changed man.

June 26, those arrested were deported to various concentration camps. Dr. Blazy and *Monsieur* Laffargue died at Dachau.

"Concentrations camps! A degree of horror that reason cannot accept." (From an underground French flyer.)

Mid-June I received a letter from Pauline relating events which happened in Tulle two days after my departure.

"June 7, Charles de Gaulle F.F.I. *(Forces Françaises Intérieurs)* (Internal Free French Forces) took Tulle thinking that the Germans were holding some of their members prisoners. German bodies were sprawled all over the streets. During the four years of the occupation the town had not been exposed to any violence nor fighting. The nuns and I were distressed to see the German soldiers wounded or dead. Seminarians were sent to care for the wounded and gather the bodies. Showing no respect, some rabble Frenchwomen kicked the wounded and spat on the dead. I saw someone film this unfortunate and degrading lack of basic human values.

"Later that day, the convent's neighbors came over to advise Mother Superior that the water was going to be shut off. The nuns, the students and I started filling all available containers. Mother Superior called *l'Hôtel de Ville* (Town Hall) to arrange the evacuation of the boarding school students, it was not granted.

"That evening, while we were getting ready for bed, bullets started to whistle around us. The students started screaming, we had a hard time calming them and instructing them to lie low. The frightened students, nuns and I walked on all fours toward a safer place, the cellar. We all spent a frightful night. Naturally, no one was able to sleep. Mother Superior was also very worried because since 1940 the convent was harboring a little Jewish girl among the pupils. The following morning, a sister and I cautiously went upstairs, the dormitory was bullet riddled.

"The town of Tulle was fearful of the possible return *en force* of the Germans. Finally, French Police headquarters sent orders to the convent to evacuate to the countryside. The already terrified students obeyed without a word, it was a time we didn't have any trouble with them.

"After the *Luftwaffe* (German Air Force) bombed the city, tanks arrived firing at the houses. Terrified, everyone stayed indoors, some people were killed in their homes."

It was hard to believe that Pauline had lived through such difficult times.

June 9, the crack 2nd SS Das Reich Panzer division was recalled by General Rommel from south-central France with orders to proceed fast to Normandy. On their way they took Tulle back. It didn't take long for the SS to retaliate for the FFI attack.

Pauline's account went on.

"The following day many residents were arrested and assembled on the main square by the Germans. By daylight ninety-nine men, women and boys were hanged from balconies and trees. Their families were forced to watch. About 149 people chosen at random from the remaining arrested were deported."

The same division on their way north to the front committed more atrocities. In a little town near Limoges, Oradour-sur-Glane they burned 648 men, women and children in their church. Another massacre.

I had left Tulle just in time before those barbaric Nazi atrocities and I was spared that ghastly sight. Poor Pauline had lived through some horrible times. In July another letter arrived from her.

"After the students had left for their summer vacation Mother Superior suggested that I help at a Hospice operated by our order located in the countryside. 'You will care for the sick until the end of the summer vacation. There your diet will greatly improve.'

"We knew that members of an underground network lived in a camp located in a nearby large forest. Shortly after I arrived a funeral was conducted for a FFI member. The Mass celebrated in the local Church was very moving. The soldier's body was laid out, a Rosary wrapped around his wrists. In the middle of the service a scream pierced the quietness of the Church, 'The *Boches* are coming back!'

"Panic hit the packed church, everyone ran out in all directions except the priest, the nuns and I.

"As the FFI soldiers were leaving, a short French officer with a sinewy build, dressed in an old tattered, nondescript uniform ran toward me. He hurriedly whispered, 'Sister, I have some important documents that I would like you to hide for me.' He pushed a package into my hands, the documents were wrapped in a rubber pouch. I didn't have time or get the opportunity to ask questions. He immediately left. What was I going to do with it? What could it contain? Father finished the funeral Mass in a practically empty church.

"Back at the Hospice, during the night I buried the pouch under some pea vines, erasing my footsteps after myself. Several days later the officer came to the Hospice to claim his precious package. I had a hard time finding the spot. When I handed him the pouch, he thanked me profusely. Its contents remained a mystery. Many of the Hospice beds were

filled by wounded FFI soldiers, none of them termi-
nal. After the funeral, Sister Madeleine, a portly
elderly nun, came out of breath to the sick bay. She
could only stammer, 'The Germans are on their way
here!'

"In a hurry we helped the FFI soldiers dress and
directed them back to the forest. We just had enough
time to change the beds. The rest of their belongings
were hidden in the unused coal bin.

"Now the beds were filled by only the local sick
people. When the Germans arrived, we all looked
normal, busy at different tasks. They inspected—
found nothing. We didn't even have time to be
scared. Several days after the Germans retreated a
message was sent to the FFI patients that they could
come back from the forest. They returned, dirty,
unshaven, and sicker. At least with everyone's coop-
eration, they were saved."

Pauline and her religious community had lived some
very scary days.

In July Paris was practically without water or electricity.
Food was scarce. On my twentieth birthday, August 10, in
the capital, the railway and subway workers went on strike
followed by the police and mailmen. Policemen were
replaced by German soldiers. Parisians barricaded themselves in the streets, 400 flimsy barricades like they had done
so many times in past centuries. People of all ages piled up
felled trees, ripped up paving stones, stacked furniture in
the boulevards and streets to hamper the German troop
movements. They did what they could, they were brave.

The following month the BBC announced that August 15, the Americans landed in Provence, in the southeastern part of France on the Mediterranean coast. It was called "Operation Dragoon." The Germans started to slowly retreat from the southwest. They didn't want to be trapped by the Allies. During their retreat, on their way north, they were constantly harassed by the Résistance and the FFI.

August 22, the Germans started to evacuate Saint-Jean-de-Luz after blowing up the ammunition dump. It burnt for forty-eight hours.

August 24 was a day of glory!

Paris was liberated with a lot of help from the Résistance.

Hitler had wanted Paris to be destroyed. His precise orders had been: "Should the Allies arrive near Paris, the city must be destroyed, nothing must be left standing: no monuments, no churches. Water supply must be cut off. They must find nothing but ruins."

But, who helped Paris from the fate that Hitler had for the city? Who had saved Paris?

Major General Dietrich Von Choltitz, the German Commander of Paris had received his orders from the *Führer* himself. Choltitz didn't want to be the man to destroy the most glorious city in Western Europe. It was a difficult dilemma for the portly, short Prussian career officer. When those verbal orders had been given by Hitler, Cholitz realized that Hitler was *insane* because while talking Hitler was shaking and saliva was running from the side of his mouth. With the help and persuasion of Swedish General Consul Raoul Nordling, Paris was saved. Cholitz accepted the cease-fire, refusing to destroy Paris.

First to arrive in the capital, Thursday August 24, was French Major General Jacques Leclerc, commanding the Second Armored division of French tanks. They had used back streets to attack the Germans. With *Général de Gaulle* they were welcomed by a crowd of delirious Parisians. The following day, the US 4th Ivy infantry troops marched down the *Champs-Elysées*. What a contrast from the 1940 German arrival. Rows and rows of smiling faces of brave GIs dressed in khaki who had sailed across the Atlantic to save us, took their turn marching down the *Champs-Elysées* cheered by the Parisians, women being kissed and kissing the GIs.

Two days earlier, August 22, a hot sunny day bicycling to town I had stopped at a girlfriend's house in Ciboure. All excited Colette warned me, "You can't go to town with your bicycle. We received a phone call that the Germans are leaving and taking any kind of transportation with wheels. They are too scared to bother anyone, only inter-ested in saving their skins. You better walk to town and leave your bicycle here. I'll hide it."

Later that day after finishing my dispensary work, I went back to pick up my bike. Colette had quite a story to tell. About two hours after my visit, several very young German soldiers had come asking for her family's car. The car was useless to them as it had not been driven in several years. Noticing bicycle tracks on the gravel, one of the soldiers asked, "*Bicyclette?*"

Colette nonchalantly, shrugging her shoulders pointed south and answered in pidgin French, "*Mon Papa, parti montagne bicyclette* (My Dad, gone mountains bicycle)." Her lie had saved my only form of transportation. Colette had been very brave. At our age we never thought that we could get in trouble.

The following day I took my chances bicycling to the dispensary. I kept looking around me for the sight of the *verdigris* colored uniform. Nothing, not many people were seen in the streets. When I arrived my first question was, "Are the *Boches* gone for good?"

Mireille, true to her nature still had nothing positive to say, we ignored her. Still we were afraid to hope, afraid to see their hated presence in the streets. How could we be sure? Later in the afternoon one of the nurses' father came to the dispensary. "You have nothing to fear, the GER-MANS are definitely gone!"

We jumped from joy, hugged each other. All of a sudden we were at a loss for words. The fact could not sink in, then we started to dance saying,

"*ILS SONT PARTIS...ILS SONT PARTIS...*
ILS SONT PARTIS (THEY ARE GONE)!"

I immediately asked Sister Catherine if I could be excused, "I must leave and give the exciting news to my family."

Luziens were afraid to celebrate, maybe some soldiers were hiding. The town was waiting, everyone holding their breath. It was not until the following day that the truth really hit them.

Within the span of three months, again I was going to be the dispatcher of wonderful news. As I was leaving town, the church bells started to ring. What a wonderful sound! As a sign of protest they had remained silent for four years.

French flags, some with fading colors, others quite tattered appeared in windows. This time, my bicycle

seemed to have extra power! Still I could not help myself
when I was leaving town, my eyes darted around, expecting
to see a *verdigris* uniform appear at some corner of a street.
It was so hard to believe that we were finally FREE!

Never did I pedal so fast, each pedal pushed sang
"FREE." My mind was rehearsing the way I was going to
announce the extraordinary news. I whistled with gusto.

As soon as I arrived at the villa's gate, without much
care, I dumped my bicycle on the ground. As on June 6, I
started screaming, "Papa, Maman."

In no time they were on the front steps. As I was running
I heard my smiling Papa say, "What are we going to do
with her? She is so excitable."

"*Les Boches ont fichu le camp* (The Krauts have shoved
off)!"

No one paid attention to my use of bad language.

Papa turned to Maman, "Félicie, finally, we are liberated."

Maman kept on repeating, like a prayer, these three
words, "*Merci, mon Dieu* (Thank you, God)!"

For the first time I saw them in each other arms. An
excited Papa ordered for the second time in three months,
"Maita, go get Michel."

What else was I going to do but do what I liked best.
RUN! I found Michel in the barn, "Quick, come celebrate,
the last *Boche's* rear end was seen on National 10."

Again, Papa had a bottle of champagne opened, we
toasted the Americans who made that day possible. He
decided that the following day I would go to town with him
to see in what condition the hotel was left. We were also
to bring back my older sister Marie and family for a
celebration.

Being so far away from the landing area, Saint-Jean-de-Luz was not liberated. The Germans just left, stealing anything that had wheels, mostly bicycles and horses. In addition to lack of transportation, their retreat was impaired by sabotage, cut telephone wires, train derailments and train conductors who had mysteriously disappeared. Supposedly, the last *Boche* leaving town was seen galloping on a stolen horse on the main road heading north.

In our little corner of the world, freedom came without a shot being fired. The Basque region liberated itself!

THEY WERE FINALLY GONE
Thanks to the Americans and the Allies
WE WERE FINALLY FREE

I had so often during those long four years dreamt of that day! I wanted to run and run around town screaming those happy words. Dance, reach for the sky, the wind and the sun.

THEY ARE GONE!

My identification and ration card could be thrown into a drawer as a sad reminder of the occupation. Newspapers would start printing whatever their editors wanted. I was eagerly looking forward to riding in a car again, to going shopping for clothes and shoes! It would be weird to see again supplies on grocery store shelves. How those delicious croissants covered with real butter would taste!

But the sun seemed brighter now, the sea more inviting and the air purer. The feeling of freedom was inexplicable. We would no longer see those sickening *verdigris* uniforms, hear that guttural language which I despised. Oh! To be able to come and go as one pleased. Nevertheless, it was difficult not to think that it was only a dream, that a *sale*

Boche (dirty Kraut) would appear around some corner. They had been in Saint-Jean-de-Luz for what seemed like an eternity! Four long years!

What a weird feeling! FREEDOM!

Our little corner of the world had been spared the worst horrors of war. Saint-Jean-de-Luz being picked for an R & R town made all the difference. The soldiers had come with cameras instead of rifles. We had been somewhat protected, spared killings, mass arrests and were not touched physically. But we were so happy they were gone!

Papa and I left the villa in the buggy, my bicycle loaded in the back. When we crossed the bridge to Saint-Jean-de-Luz, people stopped us, "Do you know that the *Boches* are gone?"

When we arrived in town many people stopped us with the same refrain, "*Monsieur* Branquet, they are gone!"

Many were singing the *Marseillaise*, "*Le jour de gloire est arrivé* (The day of glory has arrived)!" It was a day of DELIVERANCE. Outdoor cafes were full of excited *Luziens* toasting their new freedom.

How anxious we were to see the hotel. With apprehension we slowly walked in. What a sight! Chaos, shambles, furniture overturned. Papa stood in the hall looking around without saying a word. What could he be thinking? Twenty years of hard work destroyed by a mad man's thirst for power. I turned to look at him. Tears were running down his face. I didn't say a word, not wanting to embarrass him.

All of a sudden a couple of German nurses appeared at the top of the stairs. My first thought was, oh, no, the Germans are not really gone! They are going to show up behind the nurses.

One of the nurses could speak passable French. She explained to Papa that they were left behind to fend for themselves. They begged him to help them escape to Spain before the Americans' arrival.

Papa immediately ordered, "Maita, go behind the reception desk. See if the telephone is working, if so, call the police."

In no time the Gendarmes arrived on their bicycles (no gas yet) at the hotel and took them off our hands.

With the help of Papa I tore down the hated Nazi flag which had tarnished our home, the Hôtel de la Poste's entrance, for four long years. I borrowed his matches and happily burned that despised rag on the sidewalk, dancing around it. There was nothing else we could do at the hotel. A very somber Papa said, "Let's go and pick-up Marie and family. I will take them in the buggy to the villa. Don't wait. Go ahead on your bicycle."

I was naturally the first to arrive at the villa. The liberation didn't give any speed to our old mare *Rosalie*. When we were all together Papa went again to the cellar to get more bottles of champagne. While drinking and celebrating we were not paying attention to my nieces and nephew. A year after my brother-in-law Paul's release, a little boy, Daniel had been born.

Maman all of a sudden asked, "What's wrong with Daniel?"

He was walking around, unsteady on his feet, mumbling. Papa picked him up, "But, he smells of alcohol!" he exclaimed.

While the adults were busy talking, Daniel was emptying the glasses which were within his reach. He was drunk! He was put to bed, and slept around the clock. At an early age, Daniel sure knew how to celebrate!

The following Sunday for the first time together since we had moved to the villa, we went to Saint-Jean-de-Luz to worship in our beloved church. A beautiful *Te Deum Mass* was celebrated, the choir sang and deep male voices singing in Basque came from the galleries. Many of us had tears in our eyes.

The waves of GIs splashing ashore on Normandy's Omaha Beach had given us freedom and erased the hated *VERBOTEN* from our lives. That welcome sea of khaki uniforms would eventually come down to our little corner of the world. Brave American young men who had fought on our shores. Many French people, including myself, were delivered from forced labor in Germany for the Third Reich. Now I could start planning my nursing career in Paris. Again, as in 1940, my mind was full of questions. How are we going to pick up the pieces of our lives? How can one live after an interim of four years on hold.

Many losses, loss of security, loss of a normal life, loss of dreams, loss of education and most of all loss of my teenage years. I had matured in an abnormal way. For the rest of my life, fear of losing control was going to be an ongoing problem. Four years loss of liberty, loss of innocence, loss of faith in a just world. Even though I rebelled against my parents way of life, it was loss of a peaceful, comfortable, predictable world with its set of rules and conduct.

Personally I learned how to work hard, to be self-reliant and to forever relish independence. My view of the world was expanded.

Despite all the seemingly insurmountable problems, my youth allowed me, more than other family members, to be resilient. I would never be the teenager who could have grown in peaceful times. My teenage years had been erased by the whims of a monster's thirst for absolute power.

Papa and Maman had aged beyond their years. They were the ones who had suffered the most. Maman who had always been portly was now very thin. Their strength was sapped by intense emotional stress and hard farm work. Saint-Jean-de-Luz was ours again despite the fact that our concepts of normal lives were gone forever. Dreams for the future needed to be changed. During the four years of occupation the only dream had been the departure of the *Boches.*

The occupation practically ruined my parents. They had worked hard for two decades establishing a good business with a western European reputation. They never recovered, emotionally or financially.

Hitler left his indelible mark on all of us in different degrees and none should be discounted. Victimization cannot be measured.

After France was liberated, overzealous, chauvinistic Frenchmen decided to punish women who had dated or fallen in love with Germans. Their heads were shaven and they were paraded in public shame through the streets of their respective hometowns. *Monsieur* LeBlanc's daughter, Louise had fallen in love with a German soldier. I was the only one who knew. A woman in Saint-Jean-de-Luz had the same fate, to date she is in a mental hospital. She was never able to overcome the indignity of public disgrace. Many others were treated like prostitutes. Some prisoners of war and Frenchmen who had worked in German factories came back with German wives. They were not ostracized, a sad double standard. With three other European sisters, Italian, Swiss and Turkish, Frenchwomen could not vote until 1938. They could not have a profession, sign a contract without their husband's permission. Suddenly, during the occupation they were expected to think for themselves and many failed to understand the consequences of a decision to love a German.

France and its citizens had paid a high price for their release. Of the more than one hundred thousand Frenchmen and women who had been deported to different concentration camps, less than forty thousand returned. A second cousin who had been a member of the Résistance, did return. Papa and I mourned Dr. Blazy. Papa had lost his best friend. I would never see again my first love and idol. He had succumbed to Hitler's follies and atrocities.

Six hundred thousand French people died. France had the immense task of rebuilding over two thousand bridges and most of the train stations needed extensive repairs, so did our home, the hotel. France was milked the heaviest of any other occupied country. During four years, the country paid more than $15 billion to the Third Reich, yet survived the most destructive war in world history.

As a member of the Résistance, my brother Michel helped many people escape without knowing their names. We take life for granted, forgetting the people during our lifetime who do heroic gestures. They are the unsung heroes, no monuments are erected in their memory. During the occupation I had unknowingly done my part by passing underground messages and helped as a volunteer

French Red Cross nurse. In my little way I probably helped save some lives.

After D-Day between June eighth and twenty-sixth, Saint-Jean-de-Luz and Ciboure had their share of Nazi horror.

"Eighty-four men, members of the *Nivelle-Bidassoa Résistance* escape network were betrayed to the Gestapo and arrested. Out of sixty sent to concentration camps, twenty-four died, thirty-six returned. The other twenty-four imprisoned were released."

–*Saint-Jean-de-Luz en 1900* (Saint-Jean-de-Luz in the 1900s)[4]

Extend one's hand is the least one can do.

–*Unknown*

---

4   H. Lamant-Duhart, LM Editions. France. Permission granted. (Paraphrased and translated by the author.)

Epilogue

The value of life lies not in the length of days, but in the use we make of them.
—*Michel de Montaigne, 1533-1592*

During the occupation, despite the shortages, my parents made sure that we were well fed and clothed with whatever was available. During those four years I didn't lead a normal life especially at the villa. I had very little contact with other teenagers and no contact with the opposite sex except my cousins. My emotional life was arrested. Had I been able to go back to school my curiosity about the facts of life would have been aroused with girl talk. Perhaps satisfied with whispered exchanges of scant discoveries and the usual emotional experiences of a teenager. I didn't get a chance to finish my education and mature. I had lived in a sort of sterile environment shielded from contact with the outside world.

In 1944 at age twenty I was still emotionally sixteen, a teenager. I was very ignorant and inexperienced on many levels. Instead of a predictable life finishing my secondary education, I was thrown into a world completely foreign to me, and with no preparation.

Author, age 20

I had no knowledge of the world beyond my little corner of the world. It is hard to believe that talking to Maman was not possible. But, in my time and culture, talks about sex, marriage and conception were taboo. My Red Cross training only covered treating superficial problems. Whatever I knew about human sexuality was very vague. Due to the occupation the generational schism was even more profound. I had questioned my older sister Marie, but her answer had been to hand me a book. My views of the world were distorted, still on a Prince Charming level. No point of reference or comparison because my life had not followed its true course. I didn't know how to behave as a twenty-year-old. I remained shy but concealed it well under a veneer of bravado. This shyness made me reserved with those outside of my immediate family and few friends. I'll never forget those four strange interim years. The only world I knew had been destroyed forever.

Slowly life resumed. We returned from the villa to live in the hotel. Putting the hotel back in shape was an immense undertaking. Enough gas was left behind by the Germans to enable Papa to retrieve the hotel sheets and copper pots from Orègue. Happily the silver was removed in good shape from its hiding places.

"At least, it was something the *Boches* didn't get," Papa commented. The cases of sardines retrieved from under the cellar dirt floor had a special flavor!

Hôtel de la Poste would never regain its prewar reputation, as the whole of Western Europe and none of us in our little corner of the world would ever be the same. Clients trickled back, the natural beauty of the Basque country had not been lost. Despite the *Atlantikwall's* blockhouses left by the Germans, the bay was still there, the beach, and the beautiful sea.

Author's parents in later years— Félicie and Louis Branquet

My parents were very disappointed that the English clients didn't acknowledge or thank them for the chances they had taken in hiding their belongings.

Papa received a letter from Colonel Protzit from a French prisoner of war camp. He was asking Papa for his help! "He has some nerve this *cochon* (pig)!" shouted Papa.

The letter, of course, remained unanswered. Papa had good cause to complain about the *cochon*, as Papa had called him after each of his numerous and unwelcome visits at our door. Most of Papa's wine cellar bottles had been consumed by Colonel Protzit.

Slowly soldiers with different color uniforms, khaki, the "AMERICAN GIs" arrived in Saint-Jean-de-Luz. Hitler had called them self-indulgent men who could not possibly fight a war. How wrong he had been, like the Japanese. Trucks rolled down the same road, National 10 that the Germans had taken four years earlier. They were full of boisterous soldiers, smoking, laughing and waving. The *Luziens* were in the streets cheering them. No closed shutters! They came in all sizes and colors with winning smiles. What a difference from the German officers' masks of arrogance, and awkward German soldiers with looks of indifference and resignation. One could not help liking them at first sight, especially the girls my age.

I started to make a few friends. We often went swimming. One day a dance was organized. Maman didn't want me to attend even though one of our parish priests would be present. Twenty years old! Maman still was reluctant to allow me to go to the movies. I had to be very convincing for her to let me see the American movie, "Going My Way" about a Catholic orphanage which starred Bing Crosby as a priest.

Walking down *rue Gambetta*, no more *haricots verts*. They were replaced by knights in khaki! We didn't care if they walked on the sidewalks. Their whistles puzzled us, what could it mean? It was not a tune, what could it be? To the girls delight it didn't take us long to find out. The GIs' easy going manner was in sharp contrast to the severe looking, and regimented Germans. We were so awkward! We had no idea how to behave toward men our age. How did one date? Age twenty and never been kissed!

Soon Papa and Maman became concerned about the GIs' friendliness toward the French girls, and especially their teenage daughter! It was the first time that I was talking to the opposite sex! My high school English was put to good use. They were so friendly and seemingly undisciplined. It was exciting listening to them talk about back home, the United States. A far away country which I had dreamt about after reading, in secret at the villa, Papa's books. It was all exhilarating.

Shortly after the arrival of the American, the French Red Cross was asked to provide nurses for a French Army hospital in Biarritz. For lack of space it was located in a casino overlooking the sea. I left home as a volunteer nurse. I was billeted with the other nurses in a nearby hotel. Our patients were a mixture of French soldiers, sailors, some from the African colonies including Arabs. None of them were gravely wounded. It was not easy caring for them as we were short of supplies from bandages to sheets. Still, we managed.

One day, bored, some of our mobile soldiers decided to have a good time. They emptied pillows contents into the street from the first floor balcony. Feathers started to flow

Casino in Biarritz

lazily toward the beach. Others fell on the passers-by below who looked up shaking their fists in anger. What could we do?

It was not a hard tour of duty. Daily, the nurses and I went swimming in the treacherous sea. Even though I was an excellent swimmer I nearly drowned in the waves with the undertow. The sea was quite a contrast from Saint-Jean-de-Luz' calm bay.

The food was below average. The officers, mostly doctors, were faring better than the nurses and patients. I went with several nurses to complain to the Doctor in charge of the hospital. We stated that we would complain daily until our menus improved. It worked!

In Biarritz concerts were organized by the Americans. We danced in the streets. The nurses and I were introduced to American music, Glenn Miller, and dancing the jitterbug. The only dances I had previously done were Basques

Biarritz Military hospital staff. Author is in second row, third from right.

dances. What a thrill! One tune made a lasting impression, "I'll Walk Alone."

In my ward I had a patient from Italy who had joined the FFI. Pietro was blond and good looking. With his suave Latin charm he wowed me. It didn't take long for me to fall madly in love! Unfortunately, another nurse from my hometown saw me with him, and notified my parents. I was immediately ordered to return home, and I was devastated! Pietro and I had talked about our future, getting married. His father was the mayor of a small town near Genoa. Despite my parents disapproval and without their knowledge, as often as I could I bicycled to Biarritz to see Pietro. When it was time for Pietro to leave France, he promised to write. Daily I would check the mail, nothing arrived. I had even written to Pietro's hometown priest for references to show my parents. Later Marie told me that his letters had been intercepted my Maman. I was absolutely crushed and thought I would never recover.

Still my love of life prevailed. One day I looked for Papa, I wanted to learn how to drive. As usual I found him in our living/dining room sitting in his favorite chair, his nose in a book. Hearing my quick steps, he looked up, smiling at his favorite daughter. Without hesitation, I went to the heart of the matter.

"Papa, I would like to learn how to drive."

His answer was short and to the point, "Women don't drive." Back to his reading.

"Papa, why?" My usual *pourquoi?*

Annoyed at the interruption without looking up he added, "Because I said so. That's final." His nose went back in his book. I walked away sighing.

My cousin Léon's father being the owner of a garage naturally knew how to drive. I had so often told him of my yearning to learn. How could I accomplish my wish? So far not many things had deterred me. I went to consult Léon, "Go to the driving school," he advised me.

"How can I do it? I don't have enough money."

Léon, an only child always had money in his pockets. His doting mother made sure of it. "I'll lend you the money," he told me.

How wonderful! But, all this entailed lying to find the money to repay Léon. I was not going to worry about it. The driving lessons were taken in an old shift car, a Fiat. The instructor was very thorough. He would make me practice stopping the motor on a hill, start again without stalling. Finally I was ready to pass the driving test, which were conducted only in Bayonne. No problem, I would take it when I went to the hospital for my internship. During the test the inspector made me stop near a sidewalk. He then had me back up around the corner into another street. Not easy, but I passed the test and received my wish, my driver's license. When I showed it to Papa he was none too happy that I had disobeyed him. He never allowed me to drive. Léon was repaid in installments from money I could extract from Papa.

Driver's license obtained despite Papa's objections.

One day Maman was absolutely shocked when some kind busybody told her that she had seen me on the beach wearing a two-piece bathing suit! I had been so proud of my creation made from scraps of blue and white striped material. Her comments were swift, "How could you?" She scolded me, "When your godfather preaches modesty from the pulpit. You must wear the one piece bathing suit that I bought you."

"*Oui,* Maman," I dutifully answered, knowing full well that I was not going to obey her. From that moment on when I returned from the beach I would wet the one piece suit in the sink and hang it to dry where Maman would

Maita wearing the self-made two-piece bathing suit.

see it! I continued swimming in my two-piece swimsuit at a more secluded beach! Typical teenager.

May 8-9, 1945. Mission accomplished!
Silence over Europe!

Guns stopped firing, bombs were no longer released from aircraft. For the first time since September 1, 1939— Total Silence. Nazi tyranny was eliminated at the cost of more than fifty million lives. It was the most destructive war in the history of Europe.

"The thing that amazed me more than anything about the collapse of the Nazis was their total docility. Once Hitler's Third Reich crumbled, there wasn't a flicker of belligerence in them. And there wasn't a single act of sabotage on record against the conquering Allies after we smashed into Germany and established our supremacy."
–Charles P. Arnot, Don't Kill the Messenger

Fall 1945, an American woman, Miss McIntyre, a client at the hotel asked Paul if he knew a French nurse to help her open a house in Saint-Jean-de-Luz for displaced children from the Parisian slums. Paul told her that his sister-in-law, Maita, was a French Red Cross nurse. Miss McIntyre was sponsored by the Unitarian Universal Service Committee. She rented two villas across the street from the boardwalk. After Paul introduced us, I became Miss McIntyre's volunteer right hand. The children had to be picked up in Paris. What an opportunity! I was going to see the capital for the first time! Miss McIntyre asked me to find three other French girls to help me. One of them was Odile who lived in Ascain. Monthly, without Miss McIntyre, we picked up about one hundred boys and girls, kept them at the seashore for one month and took them back by train to the capital.

During our first train ride to Paris I could not contain my excitement at the thought of seeing the city for the first time! One of the other girls, Sophie, and I bravely, like two country bumpkins set out to see the capital. Our list was long, we hoped to accomplish all of our sightseeing plans.

First on our list was the beautiful *Champs-Elysées* avenue. We walked up, looking with envy at the expensive shop windows, the Arch of Triumph always within sight. Sophie and I were deeply moved standing under the Arch of Triumph looking at the Unknown Soldier's tomb. Who could that Frenchman be who had died for his country?

We took the *Metro* (subway) to the Eiffel Tower. The elevator ride was quite an experience. The view of Paris was breathtaking and spectacular. This had to be the end of our sightseeing. The following day our charges, 100 boys and girls would be waiting for us at the railway station. It was quite a long eight-hour train ride, trying to keep an eye on all those excited children who had never left their neighborhood or been on a train.

Miss McIntyre was waiting for us at the railway station. A van picked up their meager packages as most of them didn't have suitcases. We all walked to the villas facing the sea that Miss McIntyre had rented. As the nurse I took care of all their minor health problems. For anything more serious, a local physician, Dr. Irigoyen was called.

Every morning we crossed the boulevard to the beach. Miss McIntyre had invited GIs to play with them. They were of tremendous help as 100 boys and girls supervised by four young women, at times, were more than a handful. Just being on the beach was a thrill for these children, none of them had ever seen the ocean. We taught them how to swim. We exercised. We all loved those deprived kids. At lunch time, the GIs would eat with us, sitting on either side of me as I was the only one who could speak some English with what they called a British accent. A particular blond soldier with blue eyes talked about his home in Kentucky. He was so homesick. How interesting he made it all sound!

Another GI, Sam from New Jersey, talked about landing at Utah Beach, how the noise had been deafening. He could only think of putting one foot in front of the other and run, run. Not paying attention to soldiers who were collapsing wounded, streaming blood or the dead around him. He was so grateful that he had been slightly wounded. Sam was recuperating at the Hôtel du Golf which was converted into an American hospital.

Before returning to Paris, the children were outfitted with clothes sent to Miss McIntyre from the United States by the charitable Unitarian Universal Service Committee. Again, Americans extended themselves to help others. It was a wonderful experience to see these children blossom in such a short time.

A month later it was time to leave for Paris to return with our batch of kids. Sophie and I looked forward to resuming our sightseeing of the capital. This time, we visited *Notre-Dame* (Our Lady) and *Sacré-Coeur* (Sacred Heart) cathedrals. By now we felt like seasoned tourists. We were getting bolder! With our meager resources we bought two Opera tickets to see a ballet performance. Despite having seats in the *pigeonier* (highest seats) I savored watching the graceful dancers. We never told our parents that we even went to the famous *Follies Bergères.* How daring, watching for the first time scantily dressed women dancing on the stage! During each trip Sophie and I were extending our horizons. The other girls were not interested. But Sophie and I were like horses let loose on the range for the first time.

Back in Saint-Jean-de-Luz, at lunch time or on the beach, it was exciting and interesting meeting new GIs. They introduced us to blond tobacco. The cigarettes tasted a lot better than the one in the cornfield!

I often quizzed them about the landing, how it had felt on D-Day. One of them, John, a quiet soldier with a constant smile, told me that they had left England early June 6, in the grey light. He had felt so vulnerable. The weather was bad, the water choppy. He was seasick. When the landing crafts hit the beach, the ramps fell, he jumped

*Smoking with one of Ms. McIntyre's gals and two
Parisian children.*

with the other soldiers. The cold water, chest deep, took
their breath away. They stormed the beach, but it was hard
running on the sand with sixty pounds of heavy gear. The
worst was seeing comrades mowed down by German
machine-gun fire. John had told me, "How come I was
spared? At that moment I didn't have time to think why I
was there. I was trained to fight. I reacted to my officer's
barking orders. Habits formed by months of training and
instinct."

Another GI remembered that what bothered him the
most was being wet, fighting, struggling his way ashore,
running, stepping around dead comrades on the beach.
Not knowing from one second to another if he would live
or die. He had heard that General Roosevelt had been one
of the first Americans on the beach. "No one can imagine
the noise," he said "or the smell of gunpowder." He
admitted being scared and, like a lot of GIs, had talked to

the Chaplain before leaving England. Who would not be scared? He also related that when they reached a village they discovered *Calvados*, the gut burning liquor distilled in Normandy. He joked that it was so potent that GIs said it could be used as a combustible for their jeeps!

Since I had seen in the thirties a seaplane in Saint-Jean-de-Luz bay, I had been fascinated with aviation. During the third trip to Paris my enthrallment with airplanes was fulfilled. With my cousin Charles who had stayed one summer at the villa, I bought sightseeing airplane tickets to fly over Paris. How daring! I felt like a bird, free, suspended, near the sky. When we landed, my love of aviation took birth. It was the highlight of all my trips to Paris. Charles, unsteady and green, swore to never let his feet leave the ground again.

When I returned home, my exhilaration was still with me. No matter what my parents would say I had to share my experience. Probably I wanted to shock them and show my independence. With horror and exasperation looking up to the heavens for witnesses, Maman threw her arms in the air, exclaimed, "You did what? Did you want to get yourself killed? You are absolutely crazy!"

Papa turned to me with a smile, "You are courageous my little one. I would have loved to be with you."

"Really, Louis," responded Maman, walking away. Twenty-one years old, in those days, was still considered very young. I was finally able to do things which had been on hold during the occupation. I was trying to cram lost time into the hole of four stolen years.

Late spring 1946 Miss McIntyre mentioned that an American couple, who spent six months out of the year at their exclusive villa overlooking the bay of Saint-Jean-de-Luz, were looking for a governess for their grandchildren. It fired my imagination, already fueled with information gathered in Papa's books and especially by talking to the GIs. Here was an opportunity to see the world!

Without saying a word to my parents or anyone else, I pedaled to their beautiful villa. As they knew Miss McIntyre, I was made most welcome. When they realized that I was a Branquet daughter, their reservations were voiced. "But, *Mademoiselle* Branquet, you have never worked," said Mr. Stewart.

It didn't take long for me to weave a tale of a GI fiance and our desire to get married. I was convincing! Mr. Stewart would go to the American Consulate in Bordeaux to get me listed on the French quota and obtain my visa. The United States has a quota system allowing only a certain amount of people to immigrate from each European country.

Author's French passport page with emigration stamp and quota #548.

Now that I was hired, the worst task was ahead of me. How would I tell Maman? I tried a different strategy. I approached Papa and told him, "I have the opportunity of going to the United States. The Stewarts are looking for a governess for their grandchildren."

"I would personally tell you to go and see the world," answered a sober Papa, "but, you are a young girl. Maman will never give her consent." At my age, Papa had gone to England to work in a restaurant as a waiter. I was following in his independent footsteps, but I was a girl!

Forlorn, I looked for Maman, imagining a litany of objections and my answers. I found her in the family room and decided to go to the heart of the matter. "Maman, I want to go to the United States with the Stewarts. They are looking for a governess for their grandchildren."

Maman looked aghast at me, "What will I tell my friends? That you are working as a nanny! You can't possibly go, I won't let you." Her answer was quick and final.

I was determined, "Maman, I am twenty-one years old and can do as I wish. Nothing and no one will make me change my mind."

Vainly Maman begged, cried to no avail. I quickly left the room.

The biggest factor in my decision to leave France was that Maman had not allowed me to fulfill my dream of continuing my nursing career. Even though a girlfriend's father was the resident surgeon at a hospital in Paris connected to a nursing school run by nuns, her answer had been a flat NO when I had asked Maman if I could attend. The other reason was her deceit in withholding letters from my first real love, Pietro.

Maman was not a person easily contradicted. She contacted her sister, my godmother, whom I called Tantamy, as an ally. Tantamy called, tried to discourage me. Running out of ammunition she sternly said, "Maita, if you leave, I will take you off my will."

Her money was the least of my concerns. "I have decided to leave and will," was my firm answer. I borrowed the ship passage from my older sister Marie as I didn't want to be obligated to the Stewarts.

The world I grew up in was the only one I had known. I watched it crumble, and my hopes, my dreams were shattered by Hitler's thirst for power. Even though the four years of occupation were relatively quiet compared to many parts of France, my life had a GAP which could never be redeemed. Those years were stolen by a tyrant. I'll never forget those four stolen years which drastically changed the course of my life. Each loss is unique.

Although my parents' legacy spilled into the world around me, I had to leave it, and of course, it hurt them. I was moving into a new world. I could not stay bound to their demands. Since my childhood I had always headed toward new discoveries by endless *pourquois* (whys) and a vast curiosity. On my own I grew to enjoy people, entering into their lives even in small ways.

Despite my parents' objections, I took the train to Paris and then LeHavre where the ship SS America bound for New York was docked. On November 23, 1946 the train slowly departed. A world of habits stayed behind on the platform of Saint-Jean-de-Luz railway station. Also the ones who had helped build a world with protective walls which had collapsed with the war and the German occupation.

With the simple shrill of the whistle of the locomotive, I left it all behind in my little corner of the world.

I had the gumption to go after my dreams toward a new life in the country of my dreams across the sea, the United States. I was the only one out of the seven Branquet children who broke tradition, the only one to make a home away from France.

Years have passed since the train left Saint-Jean-de-Luz. I think of the GIs who fought and died fifty years ago on the Normandy beach. I am grateful for the past forty-nine years, mostly good. Thank you for all my todays!

> Home is here, in the Southwest USA
> Merci for my liberty.
> From across the sea
> You came with a noble heart
> Ready to give your lives
> For strangers' pursuit
> Of freedom, love and happiness
>
> –Maita

When they were young, these men saved the world.
–*President Bill Clinton, June 6, 1994*

Gratitude for summer 1944

At each radiant month of June, I think
of that day when the sky with its purity,
its indecent blue without blemish
covering uniformly a country of fire and blood!

Montana? Nevada? Arizona?
One could read on their sleeves golden letters,
unknown names from a far away country.
With raucous tanks, they passed slowly,
in front of our fragile fifteen-years old dazzled eyes?

They had killed, destroyed, bloodied our soil.
They were warriors, adventurers of freedom!
But us who had already lost a friend, a father . . .
With a halo of dust, we saw them handsome, like deities!

Texas? Arkansas? Oregon?
They liberated . . . and wounded our villages,
Left their bodies and blood saturate our beaches.
Like Neptune triumphant emerging from the ocean,
Their army sparkling like silver armors!

Everything was swept by immense relief,
which would drive and throw us in their arms,
If frozen by the noise of far away bombings,
We laughed, we cried, for the ones who were
    no longer there!

Carolina, Florida, Virginia,
Alsace, Gascony, Normandy, Paris . . .
they marched on the intoxicating road of victory,
write for France, a whole page of history.
Escorted by the ones who had paved the way,
Marcel Rémi, Henri from the underground!

They were all twenty-years old and so rich of hope
Either whites, blacks, Indians all under the same banner!
Forward for liberty . . . risking not to see it.
. . . Under the delirious ovations of the entire
    population.

My sons, you are learning the price of liberty!
All those unknown names, covered with golden letters,
You, children of the future you know them,
For these men sometimes, have a thought!
All the paths, the towns, the villages of France
Are open to you! We had promised "gratitude"?

I, keep in my heart at each flourishing summer,
The glorious memory of my country repossessed!
The same feeling pure, strong of my fifteen years,
For unknown men, who for me, gave their blood!

What a beautiful gift to remember
but need be sometimes forget?
No one knows! The mystery of humans
is baffling. But, today
Madame Gisèle Duverny-Catel remembers!

(Reprint permission from Gisèle Durverny-Catel)
Translated by Maita Floyd

Order Form

❑ Yes! Please send me *Stolen Years in my little corner of the world* plus these other books by Maita Floyd.

Name ______________________________

Address ______________________________

City ____________________ State _____ Zip ________

Phone ______________________________

Book Title	Qty.	Cost Ea.	Total
Stolen Years *in my little corner of the world*	____	$12.95	_____
Don't Shoot! *My life is valuable*	____	$10.95	_____
Caretakers, *the Forgotten People*	____	$ 9.95	_____
Platitudes, *You are not me!*	____	$ 9.95	_____
Four book set, FREE shipping	____	$39.95	_____

Shipping:	
1 book	$2.00
2 to 3 books	$3.00
4 books	$4.00

Sub-total ___

Shipping

TOTAL

Mail order make check payable to:

Eskualdun Publishers Ltd.
P.O. Box 50266
Phoenix, AZ 850[illegible]

ESKUALDUN PUBLISHERS, LTD.
9205 W. LONG HILLS DR.
SUN CITY, AZ 85351 (623) 875-7920
email: eskuald@extremezone.com

American Ex[illegible] accepted

Card # _ [illegible] _ _ Exp date _ _/_ _

To [illegible] call 1-800-848-1192.

In Arizona, [illegible]93-2394 or fax (602) 893-9225.